TEEN SUICIDE

THE "WHY" BEHIND
AMERICA'S SUICIDE EPIDEMIC

JEFF YALDEN

Teen suicide is an epidemic currently rocking school communities; it's a healthcare crisis like we've never seen before. With the advent of the smartphone and our youth maturing more slowly, mental illness is a major concern amongst our educational system, parents, communities, and the workforce. Jeff Yalden shares his personal and professional experiences in order to help readers recognize the signs that someone is struggling. Learn about teens and their mental health, possible causes of teen suicide, social media depression, sexting laws that potentially label parents as registered sex offenders, bullying versus honesty, and why teens feel the need for perfection. This book belongs in school libraries, in school faculty rooms, and in the hands of parents and teens alike.

Published by: YALDEN PRESS PUBLISHING
                 PO Box 569
                 Murrells Inlet, SC 29576
                 Phone: 800-948-9289
                 Email: jeff@jeffyalden.com
                 Web: www.the JYF.org

Printed in the United States of America
ISBN: 978-1986567770

Jeff Yalden
FOUNDATION, INC.
Mental Health Awareness ; Suicide Prevention

DEAR READER,

If you are passionate about mental health advocacy and preventing suicide, please consider supporting The Jeff Yalden Foundation, Inc., a 501(c)(3) nonprofit organization founded in January 2018.

Mission Statement: To prevent suicide, improve community mental health, and shatter the stigma surrounding mental health by initiating a positive movement: Speak Up ; Reach Out.

Vision Statement: to give hope and inspire all.

Jeff created The Jeff Yalden Foundation, Inc. in order to broaden his reach and scope; he hopes to provide people all over the world with the resources they might need to lift depression and encourage change.

In order to get started on this journey, we need your help. Funding and resources are required for the exciting life-saving ideas we have brewing at the foundation's office. We have drafted a vision board that includes an innovative app for mental health and countless potential resources for schools, students, and communities.

Do you share Jeff Yalden's passion?

JOIN THE MOVEMENT TODAY!

Visit the website at www.theJYF.org and follow us on social media.

@MentalHydration

CONTENTS

DEDICATION

I am dedicating this book to you!

I am grateful that you are taking this journey with me.

*I love you for all that you are, all that you have been,
and all you are yet to be.*

This book is for the young person who wants to ask for help. It is my hope that this book will get into the hands of those who are ready to reach out for help. Perhaps they heard me speak and decided to buy the book for themselves. Maybe they haven't shared the pain in their heart, but they trusted me during the talk, and now they want to read this book. So — those of you seeking help and guidance, I hope this book inspires you to continue your journey. I am so proud of you. This book is for you. Keep fighting. I believe in you. You are not alone. You matter. You . . . I am talking to you, my friend, and I am glad you are here. As you read these words, we are connecting. Breathe. Relax. You matter, and you've got this. I love you and believe you can get through this. It's OK to ask for help. Remember my mantra: take time to think.

Those of you looking to educate yourself or help open a more productive, prolific discussion regarding mental health, I am honored to have you here. Whatever the age of the young people you work with—from primary school through college—this book is for you. It will give you great insight about today's young people and how you can become a trusted adult in their lives.

I hope you will join me in striving to make a difference in your community. I appreciate your effort and your heart.

This book is for you. This book is for us. This book is for all those in this world who suffer under the strain of living. This book is for those who believe they are nothing but a burden to their families. This book is dedicated to those who want to help others realize they are not a burden and that they are not alone.

I'm honored for the opportunity to share my life experiences in this book, both personally and professionally, and to show you the wisdom, passion, and purpose I have picked up along the way —from my heart to yours.

Thank you. And remember, I love you.

I'd also like to thank my assistant, Betty Brennan. Behind the scenes, Betty handles all calls and emails and builds relationships. She's a gem and I love her for taking so much on and letting me focus on me so I can be present for my audiences. My calendar is full and Betty is the person that makes it happen.

Lastly, I dedicate this book to Janet Kelly-Yalden, my beautiful wife. She allows me to travel and speak, even with such an intense schedule. She's my inspiration as she chose to marry a man who lives with mental illness. WOW. I can be difficult, but I work on me every day. She also read, re-read, edited, re-edited, and scoured these pages for content consistencies and errors; I can't thank her enough for investing in my passion.

These two ladies deserve a lot of credit for my success and the work of our non-profit foundation, The Jeff Yalden Foundation, Inc.

I'm truly grateful and appreciative having these **two ladies** on my side, helping me to give hope ; inspire all.

Jeff &
Janet

ENDORSEMENTS

" Jeff Yalden works tirelessly to uncover the reasons for teen suicide. His material offers a unique perspective on this epidemic that will inspire new levels of discussion about solutions. Jeff's commitment and dedication to mental wellness are inspiring. His honesty and authenticity shine through in his writing, videos, and presentations. This is a must-read!

– **MIKE VENY**

Mental Health Speaker & Author of

Transforming Stigma: How to Become a Mental Wellness Superhero

" If you have teens, know teens, or if you are a teen, this is a "must read" book. Using information gained through research, personal experiences, and discussions with teens and their families, Jeff shares some of the "whys" behind the growing epidemic of teen suicide.

In his down-to-earth style, Jeff integrates information with inspiration, sharing self-care tips, resources and hope for those that find themselves battling with depression and/or other mental health diagnoses.

This book is an encouragement for anyone who is struggling, and you will learn to seek help, talk about how you are truly feeling and put trusted people in your life for support. Read this book and learn from the best.

– KRISTI BARTH AND SHERRY KRUEGER
Co-authors of *Jared's Journal and The Making of Brave*
Co-Founders of Teens Finding Hope

66 Jeff Yalden is a noble warrior in the fight for mental health. It is true that what you don't know can kill you and so his book is a welcome resource for the battles too many teens face today. Suicide is preventable, there is hope and his book is a part of that hope.

– NICOLE AMESBURY, MS, LMHC
Counselor

66 Jeff talks with youth… not to them! While reading this book, I can feel his passion.

– NANCY RUTHERFORD
Health Programs Manager
Gila County Public Health Department, Arizona

" I love that your book talks about all the things that people may say behind closed doors, but no one has the guts to say to someone's face. Especially about social media and parenting. All parents of teens should be required to read this book!

- JANAE ZECHMAN
School Counselor Shawnee High School

" Jeff's book presents insight regarding suicide and is an excellent resource for teens, families, and anyone who works with teens. His humor and authenticity make the book easy to read and the material understandable. He explains myths and facts, and ways to cope with suicidal ideation. Jeff emphasizes the importance of self-care — YOU are most important. Most of all, he offers hope.

- BARBARA L. CHASE
MS, MAC, LPC-Intern
Family and Student Specialist
Uvalde Consolidated Independent School District

" This book is a "MUST READ" as it touches on so many topics that our society is facing today whether you have been affected by mental health challenges or suicide.

I used to be "that person" who thought that this would never happen to me or my family. No way. We are too close and we do everything together. My kids would come to me if they need help — until it did happen to me and my family. My son took his life at the tender age of fifteen without warning or coming to me or a family member.

Jeff is right! YOU do Matter! YOU are loved! We are all responsible for each other. I love my children and my family, and they love me, but this didn't stop my son from taking his life.

We don't know why he did it, we will probably never know. We miss him every moment of every day; my heart breaks every moment of every day because he's not with me.

Just know that your struggles and shortcomings today will not define the success you can have in the future.

Jeff Yalden has been an inspiration to our family as we have dealt with the shock of being without our son, our health, and healing. Our family was able to get insight from Jeff when he came to our local high school and spent time with the teens and our family.

Keep talking and loving one another. Speak Up ; Reach Out. Do something. Be the change you want to see and be!

- **CRYSTAL HOBBS**
Parent of a Child Lost to Suicide
T-Man's 5K Foundation

WARNING – DISCLAIMER

The sole purpose of this book is to educate and entertain. The author and/or publisher shall have neither liability nor responsibility to anyone with respect to any loss or damage caused, directly or indirectly, by the information contained in this book.

TRIGGER WARNING: This book discusses self-harm, violence, suicide, suicide prevention, mental health, mental illness, bipolar disorder, depression, and much more. This book could trigger emotions. It's OK to talk to someone about your feelings and thoughts. If you are feeling overwhelmed or have thoughts of harming yourself or others, please call 911 or visit your local emergency room immediately. (I know you've probably heard that before. But I've been there; I know what it's like. Just ask for help. Please.)

If you need medical help, please consult a doctor or mental health professional immediately. If you are in an emergency crisis situation, please call 911 right now. If you are advising a friend or worried about someone you know, take all signs seriously and talk to a trusted adult or professional. You could be saving a life.

NOTE ONE: Some names and details are changed to protect the privacy of individuals.

NOTE TWO: Whatever term you use — mental illness, mental health challenges, mental health issues, or others — please do not take offense to how I use the term. I simply use the term mental illness for myself because it is what I am comfortable using. What is important for people you know dealing with mental health issues is that they accept the situation, take responsibility, and seek help for those issues. Whatever term they (or you) use is the term that is right for them and shouldn't be judged.

NOTE THREE: Also, for the terms died by suicide or committed suicide, I want to be fair and respectful to all. My intention is not to trigger thoughts or feelings and so I ask you to forgive me if I do not use whatever term you deem more appropriate. Out of respect to those who struggle with suicidal thoughts, I use the term died by suicide as people die from suicide just like they die from any other organ disease. There may by direct quotes, however, which do not reflect my choice of wording.

For whatever reason, you are reading this book. I appreciate that we are here together in these pages to have an open dialogue about mental health. Perhaps you are reading this book because you know you need help; I applaud you for asking for that help. It's always OK to ask for help, and if I am providing that for you, I am grateful. If you are reading this book to educate yourself about mental health, I am thankful that you are doing your part to make the world a better place. We all need to be more open about discussing teen mental health and suicide prevention.

YOU MATTER.

Regardless your reason for opening this book, I want to extend my most sincere appreciation to you. Thank you! I am passionate about the work that I do, and I am forever indebted to the hundreds of communities that have invited me to visit; I look forward to working with many more communities as we move forward with our mission to prevent suicide.

Jeff Yalden

www.theJYF.org

Jeff receives the keys to the building during his three days in this community.

HE NEEDS NO INTRODUCTION...

When Communities Hurt...

Labeled "a city in crisis" and "a community experiencing a suicide contagion" by the Canadian Mental Health Association, Woodstock (Ontario, Canada) called on Jeff. After his five-day visit, the community grew more stable and returned to normalcy.

One Person...

After a different school had a student die by suicide in the school bathroom, they called Jeff; within a week, Jeff brought the school climate and morale back to normal.

One School...

When yet another school community lost fourteen students to suicide (including three in one day), and a school shooting, Jeff wasted no time in getting to that community immediately. Over 500 local parents and teens came to the venue to hear Jeff talk; 5,000 more watched via live stream. The school community didn't have time to hire Jeff; his heart brought him to where he was needed. Jeff is very passionate about acting on behalf of students, teachers, and staff in order to give them hope and support.

One Family...

Another community lost an eighth grader to suicide, had a staff member pass away, and a school board member (the parent of five children) in hospice; they requested Jeff's help and support for three days. Three days that changed the lives of many students, inspired staff, and gave the school administrator a new passion for leading the school.

One Community...

When one community lost nine people to suicide including four teens in six weeks, who did they turn to? They reached out to Jeff Yalden and within days, Jeff was there to restore hope to a community struggling with its search for meaning and understanding.

At a Time...

There are hundreds more stories from communities who desperately needed guidance, hope, and encouragement.

As Jeff says, "It will be OK."

The Man that Gives Hope ; Inspires All!

One Person. One Community at a Time!

ABOUT THE AUTHOR

Jeff Yalden is a man who heroically embraces his mental illness. Diagnosed with major depression disorder, bi-polar type II, and PTSD, Jeff is transparent and authentic in his personal journey of self-care, therapy, and medication. He is a passionate mental health advocate and speaker for adults and youth living with mental illness as well as a valuable consultant to those who work in the mental health field. He's a leading authority on teen motivation and is a renowned expert to school communities for teen mental health awareness, suicide crisis intervention and prevention, teen trauma, and school climate.

Jeff's media appearances include numerous print, radio, and television interviews on FOX, CBS, NBC, SPIKETV, A&E, and The Oprah Network as well as a stint as a family life coach on MTV's long-running reality show, MADE.

Not only known for his work with the public, Jeff is a Veteran and a two-time Marine-of-the-Year recipient. In his younger days, he was awarded the coveted title of Mr. New Hampshire Male America.

Jeff Yalden reaches millions of hearts annually with his speaking engagements, his social media platforms, his podcasts, his Amazon best-selling books, and his popular YouTube videos.

FROM HIS HEART, TO YOURS

Perhaps Mr. Brett Boggs best expresses how people agree that they need the help of Jeff Yalden when those around them are in pain. The following is an email sent to Jeff from Mr. Boggs prior to Jeff's visit:

> *Fall of 2013, we've already had two suicides. This follows student suicides in 2012, a staff suicide in 2013, two accidental deaths, and the death of another staff member.*
>
> *All this in two years.*
>
> *After the suicide in 2012 (the boy's father also took his life later that day), we gathered a group of individuals who represented the school and the community (law enforcement, mental health providers, local ministers, etc.) to determine what we could do as a school community to deal with our loss and prevent losing additional lives to suicide. During a meeting, it was decided I should contact you about coming to our area to meet with our students, staff, and the community.*

– BRETT BOGGS
Superintendent
Tippecanoe-Valley School Corporation, IN

INTRODUCTION

Your mental health matters!

At the wise old age of forty-seven, I'd like to think that I have picked up my fair share of life experiences. I have gained wisdom, overcome obstacles, climbed mountains, and scaled buildings. Well, I've never scaled a building, but I've been through a lot.

For more than twenty-five years, I have worked in the trenches of education by speaking as a youth motivator and teen mental health advocate. As a certified suicide prevention and crisis intervention expert, I can't count the number of teen suicides I've been through with parents and families who have lost a child. I have met students who wished they didn't have to bear the unspeakable anguish of losing a friend to suicide. It's staggering.

I can't begin to tell you how much life is in these pages.

I have so much experience with school communities, friends, families, teachers, and staff. Communities that have mourned the loss of one of their own by suicide.

The experiences laid out in these pages propel my purpose and my passion and are aligned with God's plan for me so that I can assist in saving lives.

That's what I do. For every tear I've shed with grieving families, every painful moment I have experienced, and all I have been through over the years, I can say it was all worth it. The light at the end of the tunnel has always been saving lives and encouraging those who feel they've lost all hope. My goal is educating and inspiring others with the message that we need to talk more and be less judgmental.

I lived with mental illness for many years, but I didn't really know it. I knew I was struggling, but I wasn't educated about mental health and didn't know how to ask for professional help. When I did ask for help, everything changed. What matters most is that I became aware. I grew to accept it. I sought help and now I embrace it.

I now know that I am a man who lives with mental illness. I am diagnosed with major depression, bipolar II disorder, and post-traumatic stress disorder (PTSD).

I say that I heroically live with mental illness. I am actually proud. I recognize I am the healthiest I've ever been, as these days I know *why* I am having certain emotions or feelings. I know what my triggers are, how I may react, the importance of self-care, and how to cope. I live and teach mental health. It is through this teaching that I continue to grow every day.

Maybe it's because I realize that asking for help was the best thing I've ever done, or maybe I'm inspired that I went from where I *was* to who I *am*. Either way, I am proud to say that I am a man who lives with mental illness, and I am equally proud that I do my best to make the world a better place, one person at a time. So, here we are . . .

CHAPTER 1

MENTAL HEALTH AND ITS STIGMA

What is Mental Illness?

> *"Nearly one in five US adults lives with a mental illness."*
>
> - NATIONAL INSTITUTE OF MENTAL HEALTH

Mental illness is nothing to be ashamed of. It is a medical problem, just like heart disease or diabetes.

Mental illnesses are health conditions involving changes in thinking, emotion, or behavior (or a combination of these). Mental illnesses are associated with distress and/or problems functioning in social, work, or family activities.

Mental illness is *common*.

Mental illness is *treatable*. The vast majority of individuals with mental illness continue to function in their daily lives.

The National Institute of Mental Health states, "Serious mental illness is defined as a mental, behavioral, or emotional disorder [excluding developmental and substance use disorders] resulting in serious functional impairment, which substantially interferes with or limits one or more major life activities."

Most teens that attempt suicide do so because they may have depression, bipolar disorder, or borderline personality disorder. These disorders amplify the pain a teen may feel. It is because of this that every suicidal teen should be treated by a medical professional immediately and that all threats and/or red flags be taken very seriously.

Remember this: Teens attempt or succeed in suicide not because of a desire to die, but rather in an attempt to escape bad situations and/or painful, overwhelming, and emotionally charged thoughts and feelings. By helping a teen turn around a bad situation or by teaching a teen how to better deal with painful feelings, we can defeat the causes of teen suicide. Most times, this requires help from a medical or mental health professional and may also involve the teen's school, such as in cases of bullying.

I am a big advocate for therapy and counseling with one trusted adult who is a professional and *specializes* in mental health. This one person can help with suicidal thoughts and teach you how to process and respond appropriately to your thoughts and feelings. Also, if you are finding ways to justify taking your life, a simple switch in thought patterns can reduce the negativity and teach you better coping skills. If you fear a counselor or therapist, allow me to ask you this – what is the downside versus the upside in talking to a mental health professional? No downside, really. It's all on the upside. You may say the stigma is a downside. But this is your life and you want to be healthy and successful. Do not feel shame for yourself or your family by asking for help and seeking help. A tough person is one who has the courage to ask for help and seek that help.

The Stigma

Your fear of stigma is part of the illness.

A large part of the work we are all responsible for is challenging the stigma that surrounds mental health — and eliminating it once and for all.

Everyone is responsible for being supportive and positive to those asking for help. On the flipside, those asking for help should be able to do so without fear of being judged. The more we talk about mental illness and teen suicide, the greater the awareness, acceptance, and resources become for our communities.

What is mental illness, exactly? It's not that easy to define. To better understand this, we first need to get clear on the meaning of mental health. If we don't understand what mental health means, the stigma surrounding mental illness becomes more damaging. It's difficult to remove a stigma if people don't have a clear understanding about what they are judging — and we must get comfortable talking openly about mental illness.

According to the World Health Organization, mental health is defined as "a state of well-being in which every individual realizes his or her own potential, can cope with the normal stresses of life, can work productively and fruitfully, and is able to make a contribution to her or his community."

Mental health is invisible, but can be observed in a person's behavior, their blood work, or brain scans. If you've heard one of my mental health presentations, you might remember my telling folks in the audience to talk to their doctor about having a brain scan. Here, I'll go one step further and say if you're in any way concerned, demand it. A brain scan is like a map of the brain and it can be very telling. Don't discount how important it is.

The scope of mental health is much wider than the definition provided by the WHO.

I struggle with bipolar II disorder. From personal experience, I know that when I am not mentally healthy, I have negative thoughts that are all over the place. I go through extreme highs and lows. I feel like I am going 100 miles per hour and my brain tosses around a million things all at once.

My emotions get triggered and I can be edgy for hours because of something that happened, even if it's a little thing — and I can't let it go. It's exasperating and scary because I know that my attitude and emotions affect others, yet in the moment, I really don't care.

If you frequently experience moments where you feel overwhelmed and your emotions are getting the best of you, this could be an indication of a nascent mental health issue. Your attitude is affected by triggers, and these triggers can impact your overall mental well-being. It's important you recognize what is happening and what you need to do. This is why I feel counseling and therapy is so important. When you are triggered, you need to be able to go to your toolbox and maybe take a time-out, find a moment of self-care time, go for a walk, or simply ask, "How can I fix this?" Therapists provide these tools.

Mental health begins with your thoughts. Thoughts impact your feelings. Feelings impact your behavior. Behavior affects your thoughts. A positive attitude drives positive behavior, and that positive behavior usually results in a positive outcome. But the reverse is also true: a negative attitude drives negative behavior and often yields negative results.

> *"Your beliefs become your thoughts, your thoughts become your words, your words become your actions, your actions become your habits, your habits become your values, your values become your destiny."*
>
> - MAHATMA GANDHI

I don't mean to say that mental health is the same thing as positive thinking. I know there is much more to it than that. But thoughts are merely thoughts and feelings are simply feelings. Becoming aware of this is a step in the right direction — and with therapy and medication from a licensed professional, you can take control of your thoughts and feelings.

However, many believe that mental health is as simple as *choosing* to be happy, and that is where the stigma starts. Merriam-Webster Dictionary defines stigma as "a set of negative and often unfair beliefs that a society or group of people have about something."

What I want you to understand is that stigma is real and negatively impacts those who live with mental illness. The person living with mental illness believes from experience that others won't be understanding or empathetic about their mental illness. This impacts their desire to ask for the help they know they need. People who live with mental illness want support and understanding. They want their feelings and emotions validated. They need to know that they are not crazy and that they will be supported when they reach out for help.

As a society, we all need to do a better job of eliminating this stigma because we really don't know what battles others face every day. Stigma starts with shame. Shame for oneself, so it is important to have a solid self-esteem in order to overcome the shame and deal with your mental illness. It's OK not to be OK. Just don't be afraid to ask for help in order to live a fulfilling life. That help you ask for will help you think, reason, and act more clearly.

The threat of stigma coupled with the effort to avoid being labeled are so powerful that more than half of the people with mental illness who would probably benefit from psychiatric services never obtain even an initial interview with a professional. Stigma is personal.

I understand. Because I live with mental illness, talk about mental illness, and research mental illness, I know what my triggers are, and I have coping skills to help me change my mindset when I need to. I struggled at first when people judged me. Certain people still judge me, but I've learned to accept it. I'm not going to waste my time fighting their ignorance and neither should you.

If you live with mental illness but refuse to accept it or seek help, this magnifies the stigma on a societal level. Untreated mental illness is very evident in the homeless population, and people in this situation are often seen as crazy or scary. On the other hand, acceptance and action (therapy and/or medication) help to break this pattern, making it easier for other struggling people to come forward. The more we learn about mental illness, the less our society will judge or make comments out of ignorance.

Those suffering from mental illness can live normal lives, just as folks with high blood pressure or diabetes live normal lives. It's all about taking the steps necessary and being consistent with treatment — whether that's counseling, therapy, medication, self-care, or a combination of those things.

I used to be ashamed of my mental illness. However, I realize that my mental illness has been a catalyst for growth and a major component of the man I am today. By accepting this and maintaining a daily practice of self-care, I control of my attitude and emotions rather than letting them control my day.

Let's judge less and understand more. This is a choice we can *all* make.

Our Schools and Mental Health

If you are a teen suffering, I encourage you to set aside what you believe to be the stigma attached to mental illness and reach out to a trusted adult at your school. You will be glad you did. Schools can be a great resource and most teachers and counselors care deeply about all of their students. Administrators and other key staff are trusted and significant adults who can point you in the right direction with contacts of support in the community.

Students on the school's radar are not necessarily the ones to worry about. Very often, students who are known for behavioral issues and acting out are not necessarily the ones silently struggling with mental illness. School administrators or counselors have said to me, "Jeff, we didn't know. There were no signs. We had no idea." The child who died by suicide was not on their radar, and the parents, for whatever reason, did not want to say anything or involve the school.

We need to eliminate the stigma attached to mental illness. We are *all* responsible for this. The more we talk about mental health, the more we learn about it and demystify some of the stereotypes. We need to get comfortable being uncomfortable in regards to mental health. The more comfortable we become, the more people may realize this is a very serious situation plaguing our country. The more resources we accrue, the more lives we will save.

When we break the stigma, more people will be comfortable asking for help. Do it for each other. Do it for yourself, your family, and your community.

The Bottom Line: Stigma and Mental Health

More than ever, teens need adult guidance to understand all the emotional and physical changes they experience. When teenagers' moods disrupt their ability to function on a day-to-day basis, this may indicate a serious emotional or mental disorder that needs attention.

Act immediately. Do something. Getting help is OK! You tell them you heard it from me and I am in your corner.

Mental illness is an economic issue and along with raging opioid addiction, the biggest public health crisis of our time. We must take responsibility, and a large part of that responsibility lies in getting comfortable with being uncomfortable and talking about teen suicide and mental illness. It's OK to share our thoughts, feelings and emotions with others. It's OK to talk. It's OK to ask for help.

Being a Marine may be what saved Jeff's life and directed him to do what he does. Semper Fi.

CHAPTER 2

MY PERSONAL EXPERIENCES

What I Knew About Suicide When I Was Growing Up

> *"Your grief path is yours alone, and no one else can walk it,*
> *and no one else can understand it."*
>
> — TERRI IRWIN

I grew up on Long Island, Suffolk County in the state of New York. Port Jefferson, to be exact. Port Jeff is a beautiful community on the water, and I had a wonderful childhood there. I grew up unaware of depression, mental illness, or alcoholism. I have no recollection of ever hearing the term 'mental illness', I didn't know of anyone who was depressed, and suicide was not a subject of discussion. I might have heard about celebrities who had taken their own lives (think early television

Superman, George Reeves), but even then, the matter was mysterious and murky. Yet when I was in the fifth grade, I rode the school bus with a girl named Holly. Honestly, the detail I remember most about Holly was how long her driveway was. The bus always picked her up down by the Mount Sinai Yacht Club and it seemed like she had a long walk from her house on Long Island Sound to the bus stop. That's all I knew about her, besides that she was quiet.

Then I learned that Holly hanged herself.

Holly suffered so much in the fifth grade that she made that forever decision. But life in Port Jeff went on as normal; the bus just drove past her house where it had once stopped every morning. That was it.

That is how we dealt with it.

Throughout my time in school, I never heard anything else about suicide until after we moved from Long Island to New Hampshire in 1987, and I thought about making the forever decision myself.

My Own Struggle

The personal desire to die by suicide hit me like a freight train. It came at full speed, and there I was, standing on the tracks, arms wide open — staring that engineer in the eyes saying, "Hit me! I'm done! I *want* to be dead!"

What led me to that point?

When I was a junior in high school, my dad had to relocate for his job and he asked the family how we felt about it. When he pulled me aside for a private talk, I specifically remember telling him I thought it was cool that we were going to move. I didn't think of what that entailed, though — new friends, new school, new team, new life — and how I would have to try to fit in to this new situation. It didn't matter. We had to move. The choices were Puerto Rico, New Hampshire, or Oklahoma City. My parents chose Nashua, New Hampshire, and we moved to the nearby town of Hollis during my junior year of high school.

Then it hit me — what about my girlfriend? Cheryl was my first girlfriend, and I was away from her. When I think about that period in my life, it still hurts, and I remember it so vividly. I was sixteen at the time, and I went through intense pain and heartache for more than a decade.

Looking back, I know I suffered from adjustment disorder due to this move, which is a type of depression defined by *Psychology Today* as "an abnormal and excessive reaction to an identifiable life stressor." In my personal world, the pain was unbearable, and I had no coping skills; I didn't even know about coping skills.

But I knew I needed to ask somebody for help, and that's what I finally did.

When I let my parents know how much I was suffering, my mom and dad drove me to Brookside Hospital, a psychiatric facility in Merrimack,

New Hampshire. I was placed among some other teens with very serious mental health issues. My roommate was hospitalized for lighting his house on fire and trying to kill his family. I know, right? This same kid encouraged me to break out and escape the "looney bin." I did, but that's another story.

I remember so much about that place – vivid memories. I had an opportunity to learn a lot about depression then, but I didn't take it. Looking back, I realize that I didn't know how to process it. I don't recall anybody ever talking about depression. But hey, I was sixteen, and I only thought about what *I* wanted to think about and what was interesting to *me*. Improving my mental health wasn't at the top of my list.

Could things have been different if my family forced me to address my issues? I don't think so, because I wasn't having any of it. Were they to blame? Nope. They did the best with what they knew. And since my father asked us about the move beforehand, I can't blame them.

Over the years, I grew to appreciate that Hollis is a beautiful community, and I was lucky to live there. My parents did what they had to do and chose the place they thought was best for us, but I wasn't prepared for how the move impacted me. Maybe my personal challenges were all part of God's plan to give me the experience I needed to understand teens and their emotions. Perhaps even then I was being groomed for a life of service to young people. Life works in funny ways.

It hurts my heart to think of all the pain I went through, but more significantly, it hurts my heart to recall the pain I caused other people.

I wish I had been more self-aware. If I had had better coping strategies and problem-solving skills back then, I wouldn't have lashed out at others in my frustration. But hindsight, as they say, is 20/20. I truly regret hurting others when I was hurting. You know who you are, and I am deeply sorry.

I've learned that life doesn't happen *to* us, but life happens *for* us, and everything we go through shapes us. We are the culmination of all life's experiences, both good and bad. I am who I am today as a result of all of this. It's really nobody's fault; it is life and we all grow at our own pace.

But my experiences brought me here, to you. And your experiences brought you here, to me. And for that, I am grateful.

The Day Suicide Changed My Life

First, there was Holly. Then, I faced demons myself. The next incident that solidified my passion for suicide prevention and mental health advocacy occurred when I was in the Marine Corps.

This personal story not only affected my life in many ways, my life changed because of what I experienced. This event has taught me so much, but I don't wish it on anybody.

While stationed at Cecil Field Naval Air Station in Jacksonville, Florida, I met a young man named PFC Eisenburg. I remember Eisenburg very well because he always kept to himself and didn't really have many friends. His uniform was never pressed and his boots never really shined.

He may not have been the best Marine, but he was one of ours.

On February 26, 1992, PFC Eisenburg showed up late from a four-day liberty, called a "96" in the Marine Corps because it means ninety-six hours away from base. He was late for duty and missed formation. It was my responsibility to ensure that he was armed and on duty at all times, so I put him on a twenty-four-hour post as a disciplinary punishment. At 0400 (military time), I got up to see how Eisenburg was doing. We talked for several hours; he shared stories of his past and current life with me. He was obviously down and depressed; his fiancée of five years had just ended their relationship. He confided in me that his mother had left him when he was young, his father was in jail for drugs, and he hadn't seen his brother for three years. It was a lot.

At about 0730, he showed me a picture of himself, his fiancée, and his brother. After a moment of reflection, he dropped the picture at my feet and walked off in tears to his room down the hall. After a few minutes, I followed. I walked past the armory, where the other Marines were lining up to get their weapons for formation, and headed to his room. The door was slightly ajar and as I pushed it open, I saw Eisenburg sitting in his chair with a 9 mm handgun at his chin, ready to take his own life. Careful of my every move, I looked at him in the eye. I maintained as sharp of a military bearing as I could muster and said, "Eisenburg, don't do it."

He wasn't a very good Marine, but that didn't make him a bad person. I don't think most people gave him a chance. Maybe he struggled because he was older than most PFCs in the Marine Corps. Maybe he joined the

Marine Corps to change his life. I don't know, but I do know others were quick to make negative, hurtful comments, and/or rude gestures toward him. Several just ignored him. That really did a number on Eisenburg and nobody knew how he really felt.

As I stood there, about five feet away from him, I was desperate to find something meaningful to say. I wanted so badly to jump across the room and knock the gun out of his hands, but I tried to be patient; I talked to him as calmly as I could.

At this point, I knew nothing about crisis intervention. I didn't know *how* to talk to him to calm him down. Everything happened so quickly.

He looked at me, eyes welling with tears, and said, "Nobody cares about me."

"I care about you," I replied.

At 0738, as Eisenburg and I looked each other in the eye, he responded, "Then you're the only one."

He pulled the trigger.

People arrived to try to save him, but I knew he was already gone.

I wish Eisenburg hadn't died, but I am secure in the fact that I did everything I could at the time. He had made his choice before I entered the room. At least I got to tell him I cared before he went through with it.

Like so many people, PFC Eisenberg made a decision that I don't think he truly wanted to make. I don't believe young people *want* to die. They see the solution to their problems as so far in the future that they can't take the steps to move on. Eisenberg was in a lot of pain. He felt alone. He felt he was treated poorly by the Marine Corps and therefore considered himself a burden.

For Eisenberg, it was just one thing after another until he felt the only solution was to take his own life.

Because of this life-changing experience, I made a decision to make sure that everybody I meet knows that I care about them. I make a point to address everyone personally, shake their hand, and make eye contact. I want people to know that they matter, and that they are not alone.

Two Days in the Trenches of Teen Mental Health

My personal experiences shaped my life, and I became more and more passionate about how I could help. How could I make a difference for people like Holly? Like Eisenburg? Like myself?

I didn't sit in a high school classroom and bubble in my career choice as "motivational speaker specializing in suicide prevention and mental health awareness". I didn't take classes in college related to psychology or biology. Yet here I am. This vocation chose me.

And what does it mean, to do what I do every day?

I'd like to relate a few other examples of true stories that teens shared with me personally over the course of the two days I spent in their community. I'm using fake names, and presenting you with only the bare bones of each case.

1. Mary shared with me that she was raped — not once, but twice. She told no one, but she finally chose to disclose this terrible fact . . . to me. Yes, it was dealt with immediately. The police were called, protocol was followed, and the boy was held accountable.

2. When chatting with Sally, I asked some questions that brought up serious red flags. I asked Sally if she was harming herself. She showed me where she had been cutting herself and explained that nobody knew because she wore long sleeves every day. Turns out that Sally wanted to end her life, but she didn't have a plan. I let her know I was very proud that she was brave enough to speak up and reach out. Nobody had a clue about what she was doing. I gave her a hug and made sure she knew everything was going to be OK. And of course, the next step was to bring in her parents.

3. Mary walked in on her mom having sex with a 14-year-old boy, who also happened to be Mary's boyfriend. The police were called immediately.

4. Joey shared with me that he had been sexually abused in the past. This abuse led to other issues that landed him in trouble and

required intervention. He was going to court for one issue, but nobody knew about the other issue until he told me about it. The school needed to step in; it is a very serious and potentially life-changing situation.

(5) I learned about Fred's troubling death. Was it really a suicide, or was it staged to look like a suicide? The police are reopening the case and looking into it further. I have my suspicions.

(6) Rebecca received a letter from the state explaining she was no longer under the legal guardianship of her grandparents, but under the care of the state. She might end up in foster care, potentially separated her from her siblings. Nobody knew the severity of the legal issues, and Rebecca is only sixteen.

(7) Ben, a seventeen-year-old boy, wouldn't open up to anyone and his counselors were concerned. They asked me to meet with him, and we had a meaningful conversation. He told me that he and his friends robbed multiple stores at gunpoint when he was fifteen. He admitted that he likes the rush and the emotional highs associated with this behavior.

Of course, I had to report what Ben shared. Before I did, I told him a few things that he needed to hear, in clear language that he fully understood.

I asked him if he realized that this lifestyle could result in incarceration or death.

He said, "Dude, I want to change, but I don't know how," and broke down like a baby.

I got through the hard layer that nobody could seem to crack, and he needed that. It remains to be seen if he will make the changes necessary to move forward. In the end, he asked for a hug.

I'd like to say these are rare cases, but they're not. All these conversations occurred in a *forty-eight hour time span*. I hear stories like this *every day*, and they are not isolated to certain cities or metropolitan areas. This is happening everywhere, regardless of socioeconomic status.

We all need to do a better job of guiding, nurturing, protecting, and inspiring our youth. If, as the song says, *children are our future*, let's empower them to carve out a future that we can all be proud of. It needs to happen. And teens: you need to do a better job of asking for help when you need it. We can't help you if we don't know you need help. Talk to us. It's OK to ask for help, and we're ready when you are.

Families and school communities need to start and/or continue the conversation about mental illness, which is quickly becoming a huge public health crisis. It is real, and we all have a responsibility to recognize this. We've got to get comfortable being uncomfortable and talk about suicide and teen mental health. We need to create relationships that build trust and respect so that we can talk about these things in a compassionate and empathetic way with no judgment.

Let's continue this fight. You are making a difference. No family should have to bury their child. I've met too many families that will live every day with the agony of wishing they had known or could have done something.

Suicide is a permanent action to a temporary situation. There is always help.

I love you all.

Inspiring, giving hope, mentoring, motivating; this is what Jeff loves to do.

CHAPTER 3

IS MENTAL ILLNESS THE GREATEST PUBLIC HEALTH CRISIS OF OUR TIME?

Today, I will not stress over things I can't control.

Teen suicide and the opioid crisis are crippling communities on a scale we have never seen, and mental illness threatens to become the greatest public health crisis of our time.

Although mental health impacts families and communities on such an intimate level, what should be an open conversation seems to get swept under the carpet. It's hush-hush, unless you work every day to reverse that trend every day, like I do. It's heartbreaking, and I am committed to making a difference one person at a time, one household at a time, and one community at a time.

I wish I could speak about the opioid crisis, but I am not an expert. I don't research it every day. I don't read about drugs every day, so I'll leave that to others. I did discover that, according to *USA Today*, more than 175 Americans die daily of drug overdoses, which is greater than the number of teens who die by suicide.

However, the number of people who die as a result of suicide might be misleading. The American Foundation for Suicide Prevention believes there are more suicides than the data reflects because the "stigma surrounding suicide leads to underreporting, and data collection methods critical to suicide prevention need to be improved."

Whether we are addressing today's opioid crisis or teen suicide epidemic, we have major issues on our hands that point to an underlying component of mental illness.

If the stigma surrounding mental illness leads to underreported suicides, who is to say an overdose isn't a suicide? For that matter, who is to say that a random fatal car accident isn't a suicide? Suicide isn't always easily identifiable, and many people don't leave a note. A death certificate might attribute the cause of death to suicide, but oftentimes we have no idea about intent.

While the above data gives us something to work with, only the Man upstairs knows how accurate the numbers really are. We are at a crossroads. We can ask what the government is going to do about these issues, or we can empower ourselves by coming up with our own solutions. Isn't that a much better idea?

We all have a responsibility to our families, to our friends, to our classmates, and to each other. We all need to step up. I also believe parents need to be more proactive in the lives of their children. Involved. Invested.

I am a parent; don't get mad at me yet. We need to be present — ready and willing to talk about the issues facing our kids in this complicated world. The solution starts at home, where a child's most trusted adult is that same-gender parent. Family dynamics have changed; there are many single-parent households and there are grandparents raising their grandchildren, but a parent is still a child's most significant influence.

The number of people struggling with mental illness or mental health issues is staggering, and that number grows daily. The World Health Organization (WHO) estimates that some 300 million people worldwide are affected by depression.

Depression is the most common mental health issue; in many cases, depression is the catalyst that leads people to think about or attempt to make that forever decision to end their lives.

According to the American Foundation for Suicide Prevention, suicide is the tenth leading cause of death in the United States. Approximately

44,000 Americans die by suicide each year. Out of twenty-five people who attempt suicide, one will succeed. Along with these staggering emotional statistics, the economy is also affected as suicide costs $50 billion annually.

Depression falls under the umbrella of mental illness. Other examples of mental illness include addiction, eating disorders, schizophrenia, bipolar affective disorder, and so many more. Plus, I bet you'll see diagnoses of mental illness within the next couple of years related to gaming and social media.

If any of these diagnoses are ignored or left untreated, a quality life of joy and happiness could be very difficult. Is this you? Happiness and fulfillment are possible if you find a way to address the issues that pertain to living with mental illness. If you don't seek help, every aspect of your life will be hampered, and I mean everything: your health, your personal and professional life, family, relationships, friends, your education, your finances, and your spirituality. Everything.

How do I know? I am a man who proudly lives with mental illness every day.

I've been there.

It's OK to ask for help, and it's OK that your friends and family know you live with mental illness. Don't be ashamed. Please, don't be ashamed.

Society in Flux

Education is changing, and those who work in education need to change with it. We must figure out what works and what does not. Social and Emotional Learning (SEL) is a new concept that demonstrates to young people the skills they need to manage their emotions, relate to others in a more meaningful way, and build relationships in the real world. We need more of that, even if it means putting down our beloved smartphones and social media platforms for a while.

We must understand that our young people are maturing more slowly than in the past. With the popularity of social media and smartphones, our teens are not as developed with their coping skills, problem-solving skills, confidence, communicating skills, etc., and all this leads to the fear of having to grow up at eighteen years old when they are clearly not ready. The reality of transitioning from teen life to adulting hits like a slap in the face. What was once the unsettling years of thirteen – eighteen has changed to eleven – twenty-four.

Expectations haven't changed, but the uncertainty of life and careers has. Twenty years ago you graduated high school, went to college and received a degree, got a job, invested in a 401K, and retired thirty years later. This isn't so much the case today with corporate America downsizing and turning more to computers, robots, drones, and machines, shrinking the human workforce. So the question of whether the cost of education is worth the value is a valid concern. It's also projected that today's youth will have about seven to eight different careers in their lifetime. It's a time of uncertainty when a career becomes less of a relationship and more of a numbers game. Many of us are more of a number at our workplace than acknowledged for what we have accomplished.

Unrealistic expectations about college can wreak havoc in the emotional lives of our kids, resulting in stress. Many young people are afraid to disappoint the trusted adults in their lives, and will head off to college even if they are not yet ready. We, the trusted adults, must recognize this. We don't want our teens to feel overwhelmed by this pressure; we need to balance our encouragement and expectations.

Back in our day, it was a simpler time in regards to college. Put yourself in your kid's place. Year after year, it gets increasingly more difficult and challenging to get into the more reputable universities. The stress of applying to college is overwhelming in itself. On top of that, many teens head off to college with no clue about what they really want, racking up massive student debt in the process. This happens pretty often. It's not hard to understand why many college graduates move back in with their parents, burdened with almost insurmountable debt. Many say that student debt is the next financial bubble. It could be a crisis that threatens to dwarf the crash of 2008.

It's a different world in regards to education and social pressures.

The Importance of This Message

How do I explain the unexplainable to you? How do I go about convincing teens who are hurting to learn from my experiences? My "life in the trenches" has been so crazy, yet also powerfully life-changing.

How do I explain to parents that teen mental health is an issue that needs to be talked about openly and honestly?

Perhaps another real-life story will give you a little insight.

In January of 2018, a young man, a ninth grader in a small community in Washington state, was on the school's radar for his behavior. His friends told the school counselor that he exhibited major *red flags* that truly concerned them. The counselor met with the young man and called his home. She shared her concerns with the boy's father, who simply said he would "take care of it."

But you see, this young man's father didn't believe in mental health issues, medication, or counseling.

And in April of 2018, the boy made the forever decision to take his own life.

The signs were clear. Friends recognized his pain and spoke up. The school could only do so much. The boy is dead. He was a popular student in a high school of only 260 students and his suicide rocked the small community.

How do I explain to parents that he could have been *anyone's* child? I've received countless messages and emails from parents who have heard me speak, and yet never once thought that *their* child could possibly consider suicide.

Here's just one example:

> *Jeff, I don't know how to say this, but I heard you speak at [XYZ school]; I was only there to support our community, I never thought it would be my child. My life will never be the same. What did I miss? How did I not see it coming? I wish other people could take the signs more seriously and realize that what is happening can happen to any one of us. It happened to me and my family and to think, I was there just to support my community. Now, my community is having to support me.*

Yeah. I've received *many* messages like that one.

For more than twenty-five years, I have worked with young people, teachers, mental health professionals, coaches, law enforcement agents, gangs, the military, parents, and school communities the world over in order to help teens realize they do not have to suffer silently.

Our teens are suffering, and the number of teen death by suicide is rising. It truly is a public heath crisis.

Many parents refuse to acknowledge that their child is struggling. Mental illness isn't an option that many families are willing to admit, and this makes it harder for our schools to help. Many school counselors don't have certain teens on their watch list because they don't know what those teens are going through. How do you expect our schools to help when they're not aware, and we're dealing with parents who say they will 'take care of their problem' at home?

The State of Teen Mental Health

Remind yourself that it's OK not to be perfect.

Atchison, Kansas, is a beautiful, quiet, and quaint community in the Midwest, just forty minutes north of Kansas City. I have been there several times.

In March 2018, I was invited to help the Atchison school system after two teen suicides rocked this wonderful community. The two unrelated suicides were within weeks of each other, and the impact was palpable. I visited for two days, and I predicted that there could be more.

You are probably thinking that this was a pretty bold thought, and I agree. But I work with suffering teens every day. Unfortunately, I recognize the signs.

Three weeks after my visit, I got a message that a twenty-year-old man in Atchison made the forever decision to end his life. I love the people in this community, so I immediately called the school administrators to see what I could do to help. I returned to Atchison for another full day.

Teens lined up to talk to me and several waited all day for their turn. I wish I could share those conversations with you, but obviously, I will not betray their trust. However, I can tell you this: I always work with a school counselor in the room during these talks. At the end of the day, the counselors inevitably look at me and typically respond, "Jeff, we had no idea" or, "Jeff, this student has never been on our radar." School counselors do their best, but they're often as overwhelmed and confused as anyone else.

Why aren't teens talking? Why won't they ask for help? Why don't we know about their struggles?

Guess what? They *do* want to talk; they *do* want to ask for help, but they need the right environment and support.

If we discuss teen mental health or suicide prevention with young people, the responsible thing to do is also to talk to their trusted adults in the school community. We need to include parents and the community at large.

Paying close attention to teen mental health is the new normal for us. We need to accept this and understand the responsibility we all have. We — teachers, staff, coaches, and administrators — are the ones who give our youth hope and direction every day. If teens are not getting what they need at home, it falls on the trusted adults in their lives who spend the most time with them. Remember: Teachers are role models first and foremost; subject areas are secondary.

When examining behaviors of teens that died by suicide, many did not show any outward signs of distress or reach out to school counselors. Nobody knew that particular child was struggling. Our families and our schools need to work together to come up with an action plan to make sure we know how each student is doing, and that protocol is followed. We need to eliminate the stigma attached to mental illness and accept that we all want the best possible outcome for our teens.

Jeff's TEDx Talk is wildly popular.
Check it out on YouTube!

CHAPTER 4

THE SURGE OF THE SMARTPHONE AND SCREEN TIME

> *Mental health is just as important as physical health.*

As technology has progressed, parents have let their kids have smartphones at younger and younger ages. By 2012, roughly 50 percent of our youth had access to a smartphone. By 2015, that number was close to 73 percent. In 2018, according to Pew Research Center, 95 percent of our youth in America have access to smartphones and the features that come with them: the internet, social media platforms, YouTube, group texting, and the like. It's not 100 percent, but it is pretty close, don't you agree?

I realized this instantaneous ability to access information was going to be an issue years ago.

I was watching the 2012 Masters Golf Tournament on TV, and my daughter was sitting on the couch next to me. My phone pinged; I received a text from my daughter, although she was only a couple of feet away from me.

I said, "You couldn't have just asked me this out loud?"

She replied, "It's easier to text you."

I knew then that things were changing, and I was right.

This is a very interesting period of change in our society, especially for our young people. The smartphone has become so ubiquitous that it is difficult to imagine what we ever did before its arrival. The smartphone, if used responsibly, can make our lives easier in so many ways. But if we don't monitor usage by our teens or teach them balance and boundaries, this device can adversely impact their lives and put them at risk.

Research shows that teens' overdependence on their smartphones and other devices affects their mental and physical well-being.

Screen Time and Health

According to *US News* and *World Report*, "too much time online has been linked to mental and physical problems such as anxiety, depression, low self-esteem, sleep deprivation and obesity. Research published in the journal *Emotion* showed adolescent self-esteem, life satisfaction and happiness decreased the more hours teens spent per week using their devices to surf the internet, play on social media, text, game and communicate via video chats. Researchers from San Diego State and Florida State universities discovered about 50 percent of teens who spent five or more hours looking at a screen each day reported experiencing thoughts of suicide and experienced prolonged periods of hopelessness or sadness in comparison to those who did not spend as much time online.

"From a physical perspective, many studies have shown a relationship between the amount of time kids spend online and obesity. Kids glued to a screen aren't moving or getting the recommended 60 minutes of exercise needed each day. In addition to being sedentary, kids who are constantly connected aren't getting the sleep they need to function. The National Sleep Foundation recommends that teens get eight to 10 hours of sleep each night, but in most cases, they are only averaging six to seven hours per night during the typical school week. Research has shown that electronic devices may be contributing to youth sleep deprivation by emitting a blue light that throws off their body's biological clock and interferes with their sleep cycle. Therefore, a lot of experts recommend shutting off the devices an hour or two before bed."

Too Much Time Online

How much time online is too much time? I don't think there is a clear-cut answer. Currently, the research is too unsubstantiated to educate us about the time spent online and on our devices.

I have read various studies; some studies' findings determine that six or fewer hours online per day produce no negative outcomes. On the flipside, other studies show that teens who spend more than two hours a day on their devices are more likely to report mental health issues than teens who spend more time offline engaging in personal interactions, sports or other exercise, homework, reading, or spending time with friends.

With this inconsistent research and no clear-cut data for your child, you might wonder, What's a parent to think?

In short, use your best judgment based on your own children and their behaviors. If you think your child is spending too much time online, they are probably spending too much time online. Establish some boundaries and hold them accountable.

Here are some indications your child is spending too much time online:

» Looking down at their devices more than they are looking up, especially while walking.
» Without a device in their hand, your child has trouble focusing on tasks.
» Spending more time online than time interacting with friends.
» Replacing their real world with the virtual world.

Managing Screen Time

Here are some tips you can use to manage your child's screen time:

1. Assess screen time. Our kids use their devices for many different reasons, including their schoolwork. Have them keep a daily and weekly log of how often they are using their devices and for what reason. This will give you and your teen a picture of where time is wasted online. Do this together, and you and your teen will benefit from a lesson on time management and where they need to cut back.

2. Start with being practical and set some non-negotiable rules, such as:

   a. No devices when eating meals.
   b. No devices an hour or two hours before bedtime (also recommended by experts).
   c. No devices when attention is crucial, such as playing, watching movies, doing chores, and homework where smartphone isn't required.
   d. No devices when you should be giving someone else your undivided attention; you'll be considered rude, annoying, and disrespectful.
   e. Absolutely no devices while driving.

3. Get outside and get the body moving for your own mental and physical health. You can use your phone for music, physical fitness apps, or to text friends. The key here is to let the technology add to the activity and not be the entertainment itself.

4. Set clear priorities. Responsibilities and obligations before rights and privileges. Give rewards to your child. If they do this task, then they can have this reward. It's like going to work and doing your job and getting paid at the end of the week.

5. Set the example and practice what you preach. You can't expect your teen to do what you are unwilling to do yourself. If you call them out for spending too much time online, don't be surprised when they start calling you out for spending too much time online. If you are asking change to happen in your family, perhaps you should look and see if this change needs to happen with yourself, too. Don't think that the adage of "Do as I say, not as I do" flies with today's teens, because it doesn't.

Parenting today's teens is about teaching how to integrate technology in their everyday lives, while not allowing their devices to take over their lives, which is all too common.

As parents, we are responsible for helping our child put things in order regarding priorities and responsibilities; set healthy boundaries and teach them how to use, not abuse, technology. It's one of the issues that makes parenting more difficult today than in generations before us.

Simply put, too much time online has a negative effect on mental health. Less time online and more time physically interacting benefits mental health. If your child is online more than four hours a day, you have reason to be concerned. A safe zone or boundary for online use is about one–two hours a day.

However, many parents use technology as a modern-day baby sitter, happily putting a device in front of a child in order to avoid a scene.

This might be an easy fix in the short term, but what lasting impact does this have on children?

For kids, the smartphone has become more important than real-life interaction with peers. Smartphone interaction raises the dopamine levels of the user, resulting in a euphoric state. This "dopamine effect" says, "I want more . . . I want more . . . I want more."

The desire for *more* can trigger social media depression.

Dopamine is a chemical in your body, plain and simple. It's just one of the chemicals in the brain that relays information from one neuron to the next — a neurotransmitter that affects the brain's pleasure centers, often resulting in excessive pleasure-seeking behavior.

Proper smartphone use by your children is a parent's responsibility. The devices belong to you. If your child can't learn to use a device responsibly, then it's time for you to step in. You are the parent, not a friend. You need to take the phone away or impose strict limits on usage. Your children will not do this for themselves because the dopamine effect dictates that they will always want more access and they are too young to make sensible choices regarding their well-being.

I want you to understand that too much time online *hurts* your child's mental health. An increase in real-life social interaction *benefits* their mental health. Online time is time spent alone, isolated from the real world. Real interaction improves coping and problem-solving skills, the ability to communicate properly, and is known to increase self-esteem. This is very important.

The World has Changed

The smartphone is a great and valuable tool that really has changed how we live, work, and play. It's awesome, but when overused can also cause some serious consequences to a person's overall mental health.

We have given our young people rights and privileges that they are not yet capable of handling. Social media has the potential to wreak havoc on their emotions. Our frontal lobe doesn't fully develop until twenty-four years of age, yet many kids have access to smartphones well before they are teenagers. Even as adults, our reaction to certain social media posts can be supercharged, eliciting a wide range of emotions. Imagine what the world can do to a preteen?

Look at some of your friends' social media posts. These people are adults, yet how many times do you say to yourself, "Did you really post that? Now everybody knows your personal business." You find yourself shaking your head over an adult's behavior. And adults should know better!

How do you expect your kids to learn if you don't lead by example? Again, parents — this is your responsibility.

It's simple. Technology has become so advanced that society has allowed these kids rights and privileges that they're not emotionally or mentally capable of handling. Don't you agree? Technology is here to stay and taking away your child's device is like plugging a hole in a dam with your finger. Connectivity is all they know, and we have to accept that. Parents still need to stay on top of this, especially in regard to social media.

The minimum legal age for social media platforms such as Snapchat, Instagram, Twitter, and Facebook is thirteen, yet we see much younger children with active accounts. This points directly to irresponsible parenting. I don't care if their friends have their own accounts. It's not healthy, and by allowing your child to do this, you are doing more harm than good.

I can't stress this enough. Monitor what your kids are up to and set boundaries when it comes to smartphones. If parents aren't going to do the right thing, I hope schools step up and forbid cell phones on campus during school hours. Schools need to do what some parents aren't doing.

Want to know why schools balk at the idea of limiting student cell phone usage? Because they know most parents will flip out if their kids' phones aren't accessible. God forbid we can't text or contact our kids while they are in school. How on earth would we be able to communicate with them? Maybe the same way parents communicated with their kids during the school day twenty years ago. They didn't. Kids were in school. They were where they needed to be — in class with trusted adults, getting an education. If an emergency came up, parents called the school directly. Children went to the office to call you if they needed to.

If you drop everything and run to McDonalds or Chick-fil-A whenever you get a text from your child from school, you *might* be the problem. If your child forgets anything — gym clothes, lunch, money, homework, or books — so be it! Let your kid suffer the consequences and learn from it. We need to teach our kids that responsibilities and obligations come *before* rights and privileges. Parents, this is our duty. If we do a better job in the home, our schools can do a better job educating our youth.

Sexting and Dangerous Apps

Oh boy! Our kids don't think there's anything wrong with sending sexually explicit pictures. Yes, girls send photos of their breasts and boys send photos of their junk.

Like, really kid? You're sending a girl a picture of your . . . ? Never mind.

But many young people are doing this, and they think it's normal and not at all inappropriate.

State Sexting Laws

This is a relatively new phenomena regarding law; specific sexting laws are not present in the majority of states, but the trend appears to be "toward more widespread adoption of sexting laws. In the meantime, in the states where sexting laws do not exist, sexting may still be punished under pre-existing laws that target child pornography." In some states, it not only is the child who possesses and sends indecent photos that is considered responsible, but parents are charged with child pornography as well.

This is a serious offense. Please take the time to research the sexting laws (and their consequences) in your state.

I will add that many of the school communities I visit have experienced sexting issues with their students and in all the cases, the police were brought into the school. It is no longer an issue to be handled privately among the school, students, and parents. Once the police are involved (and legally they *have* to be called in), the consequences are much greater.

Know what is on your child's phone because ultimately the phone is yours and you can be held accountable for the messages, pictures, and the sending and receiving of pornographic material.

Stop reading this book right now and go have a serious talk with your child about this dangerous trend. I bet your child doesn't understand the gravity of having inappropriate pictures on a phone much less the consequences of possessing them. Not to mention the emotional toll of having nude pictures passed around from phone to phone and the bullying and shaming that result.

Where does the responsibility lie? Most kids make decisions without thinking of the consequences. Behaviors have consequences. Choices have consequences. Parents need to teach their children right from wrong and the difference between reacting and responding — and that there are consequences for every action.

Crazy, huh? It's the new normal we are facing.

I can tell you stories about eleven-year-olds who have been in trouble with the law because of this. I can tell you of young adults who have charges of child pornography on their records.

Our young people can't comprehend the serious implications of sexting, and when the stuff hits the fan, it is out of the hands of school administration and parents. Once the police are involved, your child goes from "Humpty Dumpty Sat on a Wall" to WTF in a heartbeat, and the magnitude of the situation can easily result in depression or a suicide attempt.

You might not like it, but look at it this way: Whose smartphone is it? Who is ultimately responsible? It's you, the parent. It's time to wise up. You need to know what your child is doing, with whom they are doing it, and where they are doing it. Keep track of every password, login, and account number. Check their phones daily. Make sure you have digital access to the phone's location, and/or "share my iPhone" login.

What social media platforms are your kids using? You need to know everything that is going on, because *you* are ultimately responsible. If you take Snapchat away from your child, I promise you that they have another account and screen name that you know nothing about. Get on top of what your kids are doing with their devices.

I can hear some of you now: "Jeff, I can't do that to my kid. That's an invasion of privacy."

It's not an invasion of privacy when your child is under eighteen; it's *your* phone, and you might suffer the legal ramifications.

I am serious, my friends.

Many high school seniors have told me that they can't imagine life without a smartphone. But they also honestly say they wish they never had one because of all the drama it brings to their life.

This drama can lead to depression and heartache. Sexting and using certain apps can lead to dangerous consequences, and teens may find themselves unable to cope.

Studies show that generation Z, the young people born after 1995, are more likely to experience mental health issues than their Millennial predecessors. I agree wholeheartedly. Think about it. As parents, it is much easier to give our kids the iPad or smartphone and think, "At least *that* shut them up!" (Did I just say that?) Yes, it's a quick fix, but you're creating bigger issues down the road when they start to isolate themselves. The smartphone becomes their world, and if they spend more than four hours on their screens, it could be a recipe for disaster.

Pressure, Isolation, and a Desire for Suicide

When teens experience the pain of feeling "I'm alone" and/or "I'm a burden" over a prolonged period of time, they do not fathom a solution. Thus, the seed is planted for them to want to end their lives. Too much screen time isolates a young person, and compounds those lonely thoughts.

In the six years from 2012-2018, more American teens were labeled or diagnosed with depression than ever before. They suffer greater anxiety and have trouble communicating. Many feel isolated from society and hopeless. For some, suicide seemed like the solution to their problems.

Why?

Many signs point to the ascendance of the smartphone.

As more and more teens gained access to a smartphone, more and more teens felt depressed, and suicide increased dramatically. Surveys from *The Conversation's* "With Teen Mental Health Deteriorating over Five Years, There Is a Likely Culprit" show that from 2010 to 2015, homework levels remained constant. This supports that yes, academic pressure and academic workloads can still play a role in depression, but social media may play a *larger* role.

One might consider the reverse: instead of online time causing depression, perhaps depression causes people to spend more time online? Studies show that this is unlikely, but even if this were the case, why did teen depression increase after 2012?

It is illogical and silly to think that more teens became depressed after 2012 for some unknown reason while, at the same time, smartphone usage skyrocketed.

What's missing here?

You might say that online time doesn't affect mental health directly. Regardless, it still adversely affects mental health in indirect ways, especially if it interrupts time normally allocated for other activities.

That's the social engagement and one-on-one conversation mentioned earlier — the quality time spent with family and friends, and coping and problem-solving in the real world.

It's also safe to say that a teen's online time interrupts social activities where they could be building their self-esteem and building life skills that are essential to their growth as a young adult.

I hope you are following me here.

Without real interaction, our moods start to suffer, and depression can follow.

America's teens are connected 24/7, 365 days a year. This can lead to depression, isolation, and a feeling that they are not worthy. They want to be validated with "likes" on social media. They see pictures of others at a party they weren't invited to. How can other families afford expensive vacations? There is a need to belong, and sometimes seeing friends living these seemingly perfect lives on social media can add to discontentment, depression, and the feeling of being "less than." Social isolation is arguably the strongest and most reliable predictor of suicidal thoughts.

America's teens have a great amount of stress these days. They have expectations that might not be realistic. They have a fear of not knowing who they are or what they want to do ("I am a burden"). And if this painful thought is sustained, the desire for suicide can result. Isolation brought about by excessive smartphone use can result in depression, loneliness, lack of growth, and diminished life skills. Social isolation leads to loneliness and withdrawal. Living in non-intact families with little social support and supervision is not helping either.

If we could focus more on SEL (Social and Emotional Learning) in our schools, we would do a much better job of getting our kids to spend less time on their smartphones and more time interacting. This could be life changing.

The solution includes vigilant parenting, less time online, more SEL, and eliminating the stigma attached to mental illness. Meditation and mindfulness practice can be a big help. If we could get our young people to understand that it is OK to ask for help, I believe we could make great strides in reducing the number of attempted and completed suicides.

When our young people interact with one another, they learn. They've got friends. They figure themselves out, and they grow. They have trust, laughter, and companionship. They can better cope with and sort out the challenges that come their way.

CHAPTER 5

THE TEEN SUICIDE EPIDEMIC: WHAT'S GOING ON

I've always jokingly referred to teenagers as SOS, or Stuck on Stupid. I have good reason for this, because I was once a teen. You probably were, too.

The Teen Brain in Simple Terms

"I think all teenagers feel a lot of things at once; everything's going crazy in our brain."

– ALESSIA CARA

Teen thinking can be wildly different than the thinking of a mature, healthy adult. The simple explanation is that maturity, life experiences, and wisdom serve as filters through which adults process their thoughts, but there is more to it than that.

I'll explain it in simple terms: The brain develops from the back to the front. The first part of development includes the cerebellum, amygdala, and the nucleus accumbens. You might think I just cursed at you, but I was only using big words that you probably don't know or care about. Neither do I. (My apologies to those of you in the medical world who *do* know and care.)

These structures (the big words I used) control your physical activity, emotions, and your motivation.

According to the University of Rochester Medical Center, the front part of your brain is the last to develop. This includes the prefrontal cortex. The prefrontal cortex controls reasoning and impulse. See why I refer to teens as SOS? The back of the brain develops first, and the front doesn't mature until about age twenty-five.

During adolescence, there is a huge burst of brain development, and this conceivably explains unpredictable and/or risky behavior. The immaturity of the brain helps illustrate why kids may act first and think later.

Many teenagers act impulsively and/or recklessly. Didn't you, when you were a teen? I know I did. Let's give them a break and acknowledge that we did reckless things, too. Maybe if we shared these things with them, it would be much easier for us to become the trusted adult in their lives. (But I don't mean we should share *everything!*)

Impulsive or reckless behavior can worsen if a young person's judgment is clouded by depression or any other mental illness. We have all seen a teenager lash out in a fit of anger. Imagine your child speeding and driving recklessly through the streets. While the brain develops, it's actually more susceptible to damage, just like your child is more likely to have a car accident while driving recklessly. This is particularly true if they use alcohol and/or drugs (self-medicating), which can have a harmful and lasting effect on the growing brain.

Understand this: The brain is a work in progress. How you feel *now* isn't how you'll feel tomorrow or ten years from now. If you're suffering from depression or another mental health condition, confusing, impulsive, or reckless thoughts are often magnified. That's why it's so important for you to understand that there is hope. Even when you *think* you are at rock bottom, there is still hope.

Always remember, there are people who understand how you feel — and more importantly, *why* you feel or act the way you do. You're not Stuck on Stupid. You're just growing up and maturing like everyone else.

Teens: You are not alone.

Parents and trusted adults: Relax. Your teens will grow out of this and become the awesome people that they are meant to become. They will do epically amazing things with their lives. These are times of growth. What matters is not the F your kid got on that math quiz, but whether or not your kid is a good person.

I hate to sound like "that guy," but things *were* different when I was growing up. There are still all the mental, physical, emotional, hormonal, and psychological changes that accompany pubescence, but modern teens are living in a different world. Hyperconnectivity can take a toll because they have access to *so much*. Our young people deal with issues that simply didn't exist when their parents were growing up.

They don't know what they don't know.

Hyperconnectivity can lead to depression, and technology should never be a substitute for solid parenting. We all need to step up and do better. We need to spend more time being parents — teaching our children balance, boundaries, patience, and that life isn't always in the here and the now. If we fail to do this, the crisis we are experiencing is going to get worse. Mark my words: I promise you that it's going to get worse before it gets better.

Teens Don't Want to Die

I'm telling you, teens do not *want* to die. Here is the problem: Teens live in the here and the now. Because they live in a world of connectivity, they don't know anything different. Think about it. They go to an ATM and it spits out cash. They send a text and get an immediate response. Take a phone out of your pocket and you're instantly connected to the whole world, thanks to social media and the internet.

Because of this pervading sense of immediacy, how can our teens know about the virtue of patience? If you told your child, "Breathe. It will be

OK, but you have to take it one day at a time," they might respond with a chuckle or an incredulous look. What does an answer in the future mean to them when everything in their world is *right now?*

Because teens live in the here and now, they often don't realize that solutions to their problems may not be immediate. Because they are not playing a long game, they believe a solution is so far out of reach that they are unable to act, correct course, and move forward. That scares them, and this kind of thinking can easily prompt a reaction which results in a suicide attempt.

Think about it. Two of the biggest challenges I see facing today's youth are problem-solving and coping skills. The idea that "time heals all wounds" is foreign to them in their world of today, here, now, this minute.

Theory on Teen Suicide

With all my education, training, and certifications, I've never come across anything that has benefitted my work or made more sense to me than a theory developed by Dr. Thomas Joiner, a professor at Florida State University.

In 2005, Joiner published his theory on suicide in an article entitled "The Interpersonal-Psychological Theory of Suicidal Behavior: Current Empirical Status."

His theory points to two feelings that contribute to suicide: "I am alone," and/or "I am a burden."

According to Joiner, the "I am alone" concept is a "thwarted belongingness," or a belief on the part of the individual that they do not have any meaningful relationships.

The concept, "I am a burden," Joiner labels "perceived burdensomeness." This represents an assumption on the part of the individual that they are a liability who makes no notable contributions to the world.

These feelings of either being isolated or a burden can create the desire for suicide. Over time, this yearning becomes the capability for suicide, and Joiner states the "capability for suicide is acquired largely through *repeated exposure to painful* or *fearsome experiences*. This results in *habituation* and, in turn, a higher tolerance for *pain* and a sense of fearlessness in the face of death."

Habituation is a fancy term for getting used to something.

I became a fan of Dr. Joiner as I got into researching the topic of suicide, specifically teen suicide. When you get to the "I am alone" part, you may wonder why. Why do teens feel alone? Why do teens feel like they are a burden and that they serve as a liability? And finally, why do teens feel so hopeless?

In all my work in the trenches with teens, I have found that even the most troubled teens don't *want* to die. The real issue is that they can't find a solution to their problems, or they feel that the solution is too far out there to solve in the here and now, so it seems impossible to move forward. This causes them to think about "The Desire for Suicide."

America's teens live in the here and the now. I know I've already written that. And I'm sure I will again. It's important. It's important that our teens understand life is not in the here and the now.

Teens don't know what they don't know — and there is no way for them to know what the future can hold. They are also the first generation not to know what it is like to grow up *without* a smartphone. As much as we say suicide is because of many factors plus bullying and cyberbullying, suicide is very rarely the cause of *one* thing. But one thing can certainly be the straw that breaks the camel's back.

I find that teenagers have a really tough time communicating, sharing their feelings, and trusting the circle of adults in their life. When adults ask me how they can best help teens, I don't even hesitate. I say, "Help them boost their self-esteem."

But where does a kid learn this confidence? Self-esteem comes from being challenged, and overcoming those challenges.

Positive self-esteem comes from social interaction. It comes from involvement with friends. It blossoms with family relationships. Self-esteem comes from setting goals, accomplishing tasks, developing coping skills, and problem-solving. Self-esteem is something we build every day as a result of being more active in our own world.

Three Habits that Benefit Teen Mental Health

These three things are really important to a teen's mental health, self-confidence, and self-esteem:

1. Sleep: All teens need at least eight hours of uninterrupted sleep per night. Eight hours! And if your child is ugly, they need more. (Calm down. Maybe your child had an ugly attitude at dinner time. I didn't say your child was ugly.)

2. Nutrition: Teenagers consume over 200 grams more sugar a day than they should, and studies show that sugar is directly related to depression. Lead by example and offer better nutrition and food choices. Fruit juice and lunchables are not beneficial choices for your child.

3. Increased Activity/Social Interaction: This is important because our teens are struggling with coping skills and problem-solving skills. They have trouble with communication. If their social activity increases, they will boost their self-esteem and become better in working things out for themselves. They will come to realize that life isn't just in the here and the now.

The Speed of Hurt

Teens experience pain as fast as the flip of a switch — like turning a light — and terrible situations can lead to teen suicide. One of the things that hurts today's teens is the inability to cope with life's challenges. They have not been taught the skills necessary to deal with obstacles and the challenges they might face.

We have hit critical mass in our society, and we need to start talking about it. If the rising trend continues, in the next decade we will have a 31 percent increase in teen suicides, drug addiction, and alcohol abuse. These issues factor in to what is quickly becoming the biggest public health crisis of our time. While many factors are all driving contributors to teen suicide, often the underlying issue is mental illness.

I wrote this earlier, but it needs to be repeated. It is rare that only a single event, such as bullying or cyberbullying, leads to suicide. Yes, an event can be the final straw, but rarely does one event prompt a suicide attempt. Yes, bullying and/or cyberbullying can certainly play a role in people wanting to end their life, but it is rare that suicide is the result of *one* thing.

Strong coping and problem-solving skills and a healthy self-esteem can help a young person overcome bullying. If you value yourself, you will be much less likely to allow others to have power over you.

Two Case Studies

I Need You to Help Me Stay Alive
I got a letter recently that I have included below. It is only one of the many letters I receive on a weekly basis. I also get emails, phone calls, and messages on social media from young people who reach out to me

because they are going through very tough times. It's frightening and heartbreaking to realize just how much our youth is hurting, but I am thankful that they trust me and know I can help.

The following letter is exactly how it was written to me, but I removed the person's name for confidentiality reasons.

> *My name is _____. I am a Norwegian 15-year-old (9th grade), and I need help. I just need to talk to someone who will understand me. I can't be talking on the phone, so I hope we can do this through email.*
>
> *I'm suicidal and have been so for almost half a year. I have told only one person about this. A girl, who I feel like is the only friend I have left. It's not like I don't talk to other people, but deep down, I feel like people don't really like me, and it's all an act. She's the only one I can tell everything, and I trust her more than any other person. That's one of the things that make me so scared. If I lose her, then what will I have? I will be left alone, with no one else.*
>
> *Every single time I do something wrong, even the smallest thing (like accidentally hitting someone's desk on my way out of the classroom, or the classic "wave to someone who is waving to the person behind you", or just saying things I shouldn't), it's like the thought of that keeps echoing in my head. It just gets louder and louder until it pushes all the other thoughts out. That's when I turn to self-harm. It's the one thing that releases all the hate and makes me feel better. At least for a while, until the pain stops.*

Then I just hate myself even more. I hate my wrist and that I can't wear short sleeves without worrying if anyone will see my scars. And then I'm stuck in this evil circle of self-hatred.

And it's not just loneliness, it's also all the pressure school is putting upon me. I have some of the highest grades in class, but that still isn't good enough for me. I need perfection, or else I'm a failed human being. I do all the work I can to fulfill my expectations, but it's not good enough. I'm losing sleep, time to do fun things, and honestly my sanity.

And yesterday it didn't stop with just cutting. All the bad thoughts were overflowing. I was feeling lonely, worthless and depressed. I took a rope and tied it around my neck. With tears flowing, I climbed up on a chair, and was ready to take my own life. I let more and more of my weight pull me down (still on the chair). My whole body started feeling kind of tingly, and I was running out of oxygen. I don't know what held me back, but I just couldn't make the jump. Maybe it was the thought of my parents finding me hanging there in my room, or maybe leaving my one true friend alone was too much of a burden to have to carry on through my death.

Whatever it was, it stopped me from jumping, but I'm scared that this will happen again. I'm scared that the couple of good things in my life won't be enough to keep me going. I need help, and that is why I contacted you. You might not be able to make everything in my life right, but just the ability to share my story with someone who will understand me is a great start. Thank you in advance.

I responded to this letter and continue to talk to this person. They have shared more information with me and I am encouraging this person to get help and to be honest with speaking to a professional. I feel pretty good about our conversations and the possibility that this person is going to be OK.

Saved My Life

That letter probably took your breath away, like it did mine. Here is another one I received that really touched my heart. When I get a positive letter like this one, it balances out the tough letters and keeps me sane. My work isn't easy, but it's so worth it.

> *Hello,*
>
> *I realize you probably get a bunch of these kinds of emails daily, if not hundreds. I wanted to say thank you, though. You came to my school in Brattleboro [Vermont] many years ago now, but you changed my life.*
>
> *You spoke to us high schoolers like we were people. You made us laugh and feel deeply. I have followed your page on Facebook ever since. You change the lives of people every day and give people strength they didn't know they had.*
>
> *Lately I have been in a dark place in my life. My two-year-old boy pushes me to keep going and fight another day. Your posts also help me keep going, knowing there is a person out there trying to change the world. Trying to help kids in need who feel*

like they have no one, but they feel like they have you. That's huge and amazing. Thank you for everything you do and please never stop. Help others be like you too.

Thank you,

WOW! I am blessed and privileged. I spoke in Brattleboro in 2012 and this young person still remembers me? How awesome is this?

Life is about being patient. It's a journey, not a race. What are you racing for? Slow down. Breathe. Perfection doesn't exist, unless I am making myself some BBQ and then I won't settle for anything less than a perfect rack of ribs.

CHAPTER 6

FACTORS THAT CONTRIBUTE TO TEEN SUICIDE

Difficult Situations

> *"Always remember that your present situation is not your final destination. The best is yet to come."*
>
> – ZIG ZIGLAR

Difficult situations often drive the emotional causes of suicide. Bullying, cyberbullying, abuse, a detrimental home life, sexual abuse, loss of a loved one, or a difficult breakup can lead to teen suicide. Often, many of these situations occur simultaneously, causing suicidal feelings and behaviors. Suicide is rarely the result of one factor.

A family history of depression may increase the risk for developing depression. Other factors that can contribute to depression are difficult life events (such as death or divorce), side effects from some medications, and negative thought patterns.

Bullying

> *Bullies cause depression, depression causes suicide.*
> *Are you a murderer?*

Bullying, whether face-to-face or online, is connected to depression and suicidal behaviors in our teens.

Bullying is rapidly becoming the go-to reason for teen suicide, and teens who are bullied are about nine times more likely to consider suicide. I believe many people jump to conclusions about this. The problem is much more complex than this perception that bullying is the main cause. It is an ignorant assumption made by people who don't really know, and I blame it on the media and social media.

Bullying is a balance of power. It's about using aggressive behavior to harass somebody. Bullying appears in the form of physical or mental abuse, ultimately causing deep emotional harm. It can be inflicted on a single person or a group of people, often in a strategic manner.

Bullying can manifest itself in many ways, including name-calling, pushing and shoving, hitting, threatening, and public humiliation or embarrassment. Because bullying is usually repetitive, it can erode a person's self-esteem, resulting in psychological damage.

Bullies aim to tilt the balance of power in their favor, giving the illusion that they are somehow superior to the victim — better looking, more popular, smarter, a superior race, sex, ethnicity, or socioeconomic status.

Bullying Risk Factors and Warning Signs

Bullying happens to everyone, but more specifically to the following:

» Overweight or underweight kids
» New students
» Poor or lower socioeconomic children
» Those suffering from mental illness
» Unpopular kids
» Members of the LGBTQ community
» Those with low self-esteem
» Those with few friends
» Students who isolate themselves (loners)

If you are not *looking* for warning signs, you probably won't notice them. Many of the signs are visible, but you need to know what they look like. If you don't know that your child is being bullied — or might actually *be* the bully — know that it's easy to overlook these sometimes subtle clues.

You might also dismiss a clue, chalking it up instead to typical teenage moodiness. Think again.

Here are some of the most common warning signs that a child, a peer, or a friend is being bullied:

» Unexplained bruises or injuries
» Difficulty sleeping
» Frequent illness (stomach aches, headaches, not feeling well)
» Skipping meals (especially school lunches)
» Poor academic performance and declining grades
» Desire to stay home from school or isolate themselves
» Lost or destroyed possessions
» Loneliness or lack of friends
» Self-harm: cutting, burning, hitting themselves, pulling out hair

Be sure to taste your words before you spit them out.

You would think that parents would know if their child is a bully, but most parents would never assume that their child is an aggressor. Well, let me tell you that teens are teens and kids are kids. Do you really know what your child is doing once they get on the school bus? Bullying happens every day, and your child could well be the culprit.

Here are some of the most common signs that a teen you know is a bully:

- » Friends with teens who are known as bullies
- » Frequently getting into fights
- » Aggressive behavior in school or at home
- » Disciplinary issues in school
- » Blaming others for problems and actions
- » Overly concerned about his or her reputation and popularity

Asking for Help

Victims of bullying feel helpless and alone. This makes it difficult to ask for help, because they are admitting that they are powerless over their aggressor. Often, the victim doesn't want anybody else to know what they are going through for fear that they will be perceived as weak — causing any would-be confidants to think less of them.

Bullying is about dominance and power, and often victims don't want to speak up because they are afraid of potential backlash from the bully or from their peers. The goal of bullying is to humiliate, causing victims to feel worthless. Many teens downplay what might really be happening, and those around them might think everything is fine — but underneath this façade is a hurting teenager who feels helpless.

Bullying can lead to sadness and insecurity. It can result in low self-esteem, depression, self-harm, and isolation. The victim becomes anxious and afraid to go to school and may entertain thoughts of suicide as the only way out.

Talking to a trusted adult, a person who understands both the dynamics of suicide and the psychology behind it, can be of great help. If you or someone you know is being physically harmed, go directly to the police and file a report. I suggest keeping a journal and reporting what is happening to school administrators — especially if you witness bullying on school property, the school bus, or at school events.

If bullying takes place outside of school, there is little the school can do. This issue becomes more about parenting. Bullying laws haven't caught up yet. There is progress on many levels, but not as much or as quickly as we would hope.

Parents: If you suspect your child is being bullied online, take away devices. If they need a computer for homework, make sure they sit at the dining room table where you can monitor their activity. Make sure your child stays off social media. Eliminate the need for them to be online.

Teens: If you are the victim of bullying, whether in person or online, you need to speak up and tell someone. We can't help you if nobody knows what you are going through. Young people need to spend time offline and ignore abuse that happens behind a screen. Ignore. Ignore. Ignore.

Cyberbullying

Because our kids are constantly connected, it's almost impossible to avoid an encounter with a cyberbully. The more we live our lives online, the greater impact this will have on our well-being.

Cyberbullying, as the name implies, takes place online — and it's brutal.

Cyberbullying happens on social media, text messages, group chats, or any other form of digital communication. It is hidden from the real world by a screen, but its implications are widespread. People receive threats online, often anonymously, and cyberbullies use social media to publicly humiliate or attack their victims — with their words, made up stories, rumors, photos of the victim taken without consent, tagging others, and so much more.

Sometimes teens end up cyberbullying just to be "funny," and they don't realize the impact their words can have. So talk with your teen about this.

Cyberbullying Statistics

> *"Bullying victims are 9 times more likely to commit suicide.*
> *A keyboard away doesn't make it okay."*
> - ANTI-BULLYING QUOTE

Bullying statistics show that cyberbullying is a serious problem among teens. By being more aware of cyberbullying, teens and adults can help to fight it. The statistics are more frightening than we realize, and they need to be talked about and addressed.

You can read the statistics here: Anti-Bullying Help, Facts, and More. http://www.bullyingstatistics.org/content/cyber-bullying-statistics.html

Being Too Sensitive

I strongly believe that we've become too soft as a society, and that most parents don't help the situation. Bullying isn't new. It has probably been an issue since one caveman learned that he could intimidate other cavemen. I'm not saying it's right, but we need to gain some perspective. We need to understand that what someone perceives as bullying might not be bullying at all. If someone says something to you that hurts your feelings, you can't automatically assume that you're being bullied. There is a difference in being mean and being a bully.

Let's say your son is in the seventh grade and he doesn't like to shower. He showers maybe once every three days and just uses Axe body spray between showers. This does not take the place of good old-fashioned soap and water, but he thinks he's good to go.

In school, some other kid walks up to him and says, "Dude, you smell."

Your son comes home all upset because some other kid told him that he smells, and he is visibly shaken.

You ask, "Honey, what's wrong?"

Your son replies, "They're making fun of me at school."

As a parent, you immediately spring into protective mode. You are up in arms because your son is being made fun of at school, but he hasn't given you the whole story. You automatically go into the default that no child should be made fun of. In reality, the other kid told your son something he needed to hear. No matter the other kid's intentions, he actually helped your son. Ask for details. Find out what was said. There are always two sides to a story.

It turns out that your son smells. He needs a shower. As the parent, you need to enforce it. Send him upstairs, turn the water on and tell him, "Get in that shower. Use soap and water, wash your hair and rinse off."

Your son needs to realize that people aren't saying this *to* him. They are saying it *for* him. We need to be a little less sensitive and realize that just because a teacher, coach, or another parent says something, we don't have to assume that they are being mean. They may be trying to help. Are there mean people? Of course! There are jerks out there, but there are also people who tell it like it is. Are they necessarily bullies? I don't think so.

You're Fat!

> *"Honesty is the first chapter in the book of wisdom."*
>
> - THOMAS JEFFERSON

In 2016, I underwent a major spinal cord fusion. This triggered a deep depression which spiraled out of control. Because of this surgery, I lost my voice — and in effect, my livelihood — for six months. I was under doctor's orders to stay in my house so that I could recover without injuring myself further. I lost my identity, sunk deeper into major depression, and my diabetes went crazy. I was in rough shape.

After a hospital stay caused by my diabetes, I decided to see a counselor. She put me on medication for depression. In the hospital, I knew that my health was in a serious tailspin. The doctor came into my room and told me I was going to die. At any moment, something catastrophic could happen that would result in my death.

I had a choice. I could listen to the doctor and turn my life around, or I could continue living in total disregard for my health, which would send me to an early grave. Do you think I listened? Of course I didn't.

Why is it that we sometimes don't listen until we have to?

My day of reckoning came one night as I was walking through Chicago O'Hare International Airport and searing pain cut through both of my feet into my lower back. The pain was so intense that I cried. To make matters worse, not one person came to me to see if I needed help. Nobody.

For the next seven months, I bounced from foot doctor to back doctor in a seemingly endless cycle, with each doctor passing the proverbial buck to the other. I was told, "It's not your feet, Mr. Yalden, it's your back" by the foot doctor, and "It's not your back, Mr. Yalden, it's your feet" by the back doctor.

I was at my wits' end, with no apparent solution in sight.

Finally, after seven months, the doctors decided that I needed a nerve conduction test. Why didn't they choose to do this from the beginning? I don't know for sure, but I chalk it up as just another flaw in our already broken medical and health insurance system. It sucks.

After my nerve conduction test, the doctor came in to give me my results.

"Ah, Mr. Yalden. You know why you are having so much pain?"

If I knew the answer to that question, would I be sitting there?

"Why, doc?" I asked.

"You're fat," he said.

What? Who the hell was he to tell me I was fat? Where was his sensitivity? A medical professional is supposed to have some sort of bedside manner, right?

This doctor told me something I needed to hear and it was probably my last chance. I could dwell on the perceived insult, or I could take it at face value. He needed to tell me something important in a way that I would actually hear and process what he said.

It took that doctor telling me I was fat to make me quit living in denial. I needed to stop looking in the mirror and saying to myself, "I'm not fat, I play football." I was forty-five years old at the time. At what point do you stop looking in the mirror, telling yourself that you play football, when that boat sailed decades earlier?

Are you getting what I am saying here? When that doctor told me I was fat, that was the catalyst I needed to make the changes I needed to make — not just to survive, but to thrive. The lifestyle changes I made were radical, and I am proud to report that I am currently free from diabetes and have lost more than a hundred pounds. In the space of two years, my A1C numbers went from 15.5 to 6.0, blood sugar levels dropped from over 550 to 90, and my triglycerides fell from a dangerous 2784 to 220.

To the doctor who told me what I needed to hear: Thank you!

It's not what happens *to* us that counts. It is how we *react* to what happens that matters in our lives. Next time you think you are being bullied when somebody says something, I want you to step back and consider this: Is this person being a jerk or are they saying something that you need to hear?

Of course, there is *real* bullying. It's wrong and should never be tolerated.

Some of our young people have a hard time communicating, and that is often reflected in their tone. Perhaps it's a sarcastic edge that you don't get, or a conversational style that doesn't play well for you. And remember, what might be perceived as bullying might actually be a person saying something that could help you.

Let's all work on being a little less sensitive. This goes for teens as well as parents. And we can all benefit from more kindness.

Dude. Be nice.

People who can't be nice are often lonely and hateful. They probably don't want you in their circle of friends. Do you *really* want to be in that circle anyway? Concentrate on being your best self, and let what people say and think roll off your shoulders. Let their words come in one ear and go out the other.

Ignore. Ignore. Ignore. Don't allow anyone to have power over you and your emotions. You matter. What you think of yourself matters.

Lastly, if you are that kid who hasn't showered in three days, go get in the shower now and put soap and water where it needs to go.

Loneliness

Being a teenager is one of the most difficult phases of life. Many teenagers feel alone, isolated, or somehow set apart. Many teens experience these feelings occasionally, as this is part of growing up and maturing, but some teens need help and may refuse to admit that they need help. Here again, think about the smartphone and the isolation of today's youth who are spending more and more time on their phones with less and less social interaction.

They need help. They really do. Everybody needs help at times — whether it's grief counseling after a death, marriage counseling to learn how to communicate better, or therapy to deal with a mental illness. Most of the time, we convince ourselves that we can manage everything on our own, but in reality, we can't.

When they feel alone, what do teenagers do? They open up their phones, computers, or tablets. They fire up the internet and social media platforms or text a friend, hoping that someone cares about them. There is a strong desire that others will give them support and appreciate them for who they are.

Parents don't understand teen problems, even if they think they do. The internet, social media, texting, and YouTube are where teens go to find something — the passion that they lost or the happiness that they need. They are looking for connection and acceptance.

It's not that our teens think happiness is available on the internet, but it's a distraction from what they're feeling. This distraction is very useful when they are feeling lonely. Imagine that they go online and find someone their same age, dealing with the same issues that they are. It's comforting for them to know that they are not the only one having that particular problem. You can see their point of view.

Some teens wonder, Why can't we have long-term and lasting friends?

People talk behind our backs, especially the ones we thought were our friends. While this has gone on in every generation, social media can make gossip and back-biting more immediate and painful. Adolescence is always an unsettling time, with many physical, emotional, psychological, and social changes that accompany this stage of life. Some teens feel more comfortable with their online friends — virtual friends that they wish were real and sitting right beside them.

Why Teens Feel Alone:

- » Family problems
- » No real friends (just faces who pretend to be)
- » No acceptance in society (as a whole or in smaller groups like schools or with peers)
- » Not satisfied with life
- » Nobody understands them
- » Not accepted for their choices (music artists/genre, fashion style, personality, sexual orientation, political affiliation)
- » Prejudices (some people find it fun to criticize you)
- » Rumors (it's difficult to stop them)
- » Being afraid to speak up (sharing of opinions becomes difficult, and you get trapped by your own self-doubt)

There are so many more reasons. The list can go on and on.

Appearances Versus Reality

There are many changes in life that teens tend to embrace. Many are anxious to grow up, get their driver's licenses, and start their adult lives. There are other types of changes that teens don't always welcome. When something is different, they try to change it back to normal. But what is normal these days?

Young people may struggle with their changing physical appearance or desire to be attractive. They try new things, they want to make a good impression, and they want to make lasting and positive changes for themselves. Teens run the risk of being judged or ridiculed and often they are not accepted for who they really are.

Hopeless and Helpless

Most teens interviewed after a suicide attempt say that feelings of hopelessness and helplessness prompted them to try to take their lives. Suicidal teens often feel like they are in situations that have no solutions. They see no way out but death. Teens often feel they lack the power and control to change their situations.

Other emotional causes come from trying to escape feelings of pain, rejection, hurt, being unloved, victimization, or loss — that their feelings are unbearable and will never end. They think the only way of escape is suicide. They get to the point where they've justified it enough to where it makes sense and they're doing their loved ones a favor.

Being a Burden and Failed Expectations

Unrealistic academic, social, or family expectations can create a strong sense of rejection and can lead to deep disappointment. When things go wrong at school or at home, teens often overreact. Many young people feel that life is not fair or that things "never go their way." They feel stressed out and confused.

To make matters worse, teens are bombarded by conflicting messages from parents, friends, and society at large. Modern teens are exposed to more of what life has to offer — both good and bad — on television, at school, in magazines, and on the internet.

Dealing with Adolescent Pressures

When teens feel down, there are ways they can cope with these feelings to avoid serious depression. The following suggestions can help develop the sense of acceptance and belonging that is so important to adolescents.

» Try to make new friends. Healthy relationships with peers are central to a teen's self-esteem and provide an important social outlet.
» Participate in sports, a job, school activities, or hobbies. Staying busy helps teens focus on positive activities rather than negative feelings, behaviors, or peer pressure.
» Join organizations that offer programs for young people. There is a myriad of social programs geared to the needs of teens to help develop additional interests.

» Ask a trusted adult for help. When problems seem too much to handle alone, teens should not be afraid to ask for help, but adults need to be present for teens without lecturing or making them feel that their emotions aren't justified.

But sometimes, despite everyone's best efforts, teens become depressed. Many factors can contribute to depression. Studies show that some depressed people have too much or too little of certain brain chemicals that can affect moods, emotions, and/or perception.

Disturbing Media

It's amazing how much information our teens have access to on the internet, some of which can be traumatizing. In addition to cyberbullying, kids can now easily access information about how to hurt themselves or how to harm others.

Modern media continues to become more sophisticated and graphic in content, exposing our teens to many potentially negative and dangerous influences. The internet allows our teens to visualize more of the world's evil than their parents ever could have imagined a generation ago.

Expectation to Be Number One

We've really set a high bar for our youth in today's society which causes them to feel stressed, like a burden, and possibly like a disappointment.

We continue to set these unrealistic expectations without understanding how much the world has changed for today's young people. Unrealistic expectations have a negative impact and can lead to further crises in your teen's overall mental well-being. This is an epidemic, America — WAKE UP!

Part of my job involves my reading suicide notes and the journals of young people who've died by suicide. One of most common themes I've read this year is failing in the desire to be perfect. Perfect! What and who is perfect? Something causes our teens to feel that if they're not perfect, then what is the point?

"Children who feel secure, without feeling controlled, have less to rebel against in the teen years and may be more comfortable managing their own lives as adults," writes author and physician Kenneth Ginsburg in his book, *Raising Kids to Thrive*.

Dr. Ellen Rome of the Cleveland Clinic provides a variety of tips for adults to help struggling teens:

» Don't hover over them and fix every little thing that goes wrong. Be present and "committed to helping him or her ride the ups and downs of life."

» Praise effort and don't solely focus on the outcome. If your child is only praised based on the outcome, like a score on a test, they "may become afraid of causing disappointment compared to the child praised for what they did" to get to where they are.

» Use more words that support and encourage when disciplining your child. "Praise them for what they did correctly *and* add your expectations to correct what they failed to do." When disciplining them, before you expect your child to understand where you are coming from, you must also listen to where they are coming from. Listen.

» Validate your child for their feelings and let them know these feelings will be their strength someday and will help them. Empathy and feelings are not wrong.

» Let your child know that speaking to a trusted adult in their life is not a weakness and you support being open and honest. If you are resistant to seeking outside help, "they will read your mixed emotions and possibly feel ashamed or resistant to help."

» "Develop a code word that [your family uses when your child is in an uncomfortable] situation and they need to leave. Allow the child to shift the blame to the mean mom or dad as a reason to leave." No questions asked and praise them for not wanting to be in a situation they know they shouldn't be in.

» Always check in with your child when they get home. This way if they know you'll be present and asking questions (smell or sense), this could "help them create their own boundaries."

» Let dinnertime be a time for family where you can be a great example and a role model. Have conversations about the good part of your day as well as what wasn't so good. Talk about the most meaningful moment and something embarrassing that may have happened. Talk and also listen. Be a family and enjoy this time without the devices.

The Desire to Die

The pain from thinking they're alone or they are a burden, or the pressure that a situation is overwhelming, builds up over a period of time. These things can become unbearable, so much so that suicide seems to be the best option. Again, teens don't *want* to die, but too many teens are in a lot of pain — and far too many of them choose not to reach out for help. Some believe there is no help, and therefore, no hope.

I met a sixteen-year-old in Indiana shortly after her failed suicide attempt. After about twenty minutes with her and the school counselor I asked her why she didn't ask for help when she knew she needed help. Her reply? "Nobody asked me."

WOW! How are we supposed to help our teens if we don't know our teens need help? Teens have to be comfortable asking for help, but that will only happen when we, the trusted adults, make them feel comfortable. This way, they can speak without fear of judgment — secure in the fact that their feelings and emotions will be validated.

Jeff is interactive; always asking questions of his audience.

Jeff exposes truth. This is where we grow. The mirror is that place of self-actualization.

As close friends mourn the loss of a loved one, Jeff listens, validates their thoughts and feelings, and gives hope.

Jeff teaches Theory on Teen Suicide to a school community following a loss.

Jeff is always present when talking to students during his full day school or community visits.

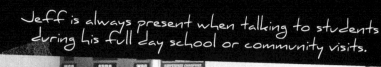

Big audiences or small, Jeff speaks from his heart. Always.

The T-Man's 5K Run/Walk raised over $24,000 for The Jeff Yalden Foundation, Inc.

Jeff talks teen mental health and suicide prevention with a small group of students.

CHAPTER 7

DEPRESSION

What is Depression?

You are not too broken to be healed.

Depression is an intense feeling of sadness sustained over a period of two weeks or more without a break. Specifically, if you have four or more of the symptoms of depression listed below that last two weeks or more, that is a major red flag. You need to talk to your doctor because you may have depression. If you are a parent and notice four or more of these symptoms in your teen, it is time to intervene.

I strongly urge you to take all signs seriously and have a mental health professional diagnose your child. Too many times I've heard a parent blame adverse behavior on teen years, hormones, etc. Please take all signs seriously.

Symptoms of Depression:

- » Withdrawing from family and friends
- » Losing interest in social and extracurricular activities
- » Lack of energy
- » Feeling tired most of the time
- » Anxiety
- » Irritability
- » Anger
- » Feelings of sadness for a prolonged period of the time
- » Significant weight fluctuations
- » Sleep pattern changes
- » Physical pains, aches, or sickness, even though there may not be anything physically wrong
- » Indifference about the future
- » Fear of being a burden
- » Uncharacteristic pessimism
- » Feelings of guilt
- » Lowered self-esteem
- » Suicidal thoughts

Depression can be debilitating. It can also cloud your judgment and impair your ability to see solutions to what are likely temporary problems. I've heard depression described as wearing sunglasses in an already dark room. It completely distorts your thinking and creates feelings of failure and disappointment, where everything is negative and sad. It's like walking through sludge — slowing you down and causing you not to want to move forward.

I can get all clinical here and talk about major depression, dysthymia, bipolar disorder, and more, but my point is that many of our teens are already well aware that they may be depressed. The emotional pain they may endure in the here and now is intense. It is important for the adults in their lives to understand that and react immediately.

While an adult may see a problem as temporary, a teen might see it as the end of the world. Many teens haven't been encouraged to overcome obstacles and lack the coping and problem-solving skills necessary to get through the challenges that come their way. It seems they have lost the ability to communicate due to the advent of the smartphone.

From Eleven to Twenty-Four: A Very Unsettling Time for Youth

I used to say that a very unsettling and risky time for our young people was between the ages of thirteen and nineteen, but with what I have seen since the surge of smartphones and social media, this gamut has changed. A more accurate range is between the ages of eleven to twenty-four. Our kids are exposed to adult subjects at a younger age, but they're maturing later. Even at the high end of this range, I have seen that many young people are still unclear about what "adulting" means.

Add the internet, constant connectivity, and social media platforms to the normal physical and emotional changes that accompany this stage of life, and it becomes clear that these young people are at risk of becoming depressed. We need to be vigilant and watch for signs.

Causes of Teen Depression

Ups and downs are a regular part of adolescence, but when the "down" periods last longer than usual, this could be the result of an unbalance of chemicals in the brain called neurotransmitters.

Kendra Cherry on the site verywellmind.com states, "A neurotransmitter is defined as a chemical messenger that carries, boosts, and balances signals between neurons, or nerve cells, and other cells in the body. These chemical messengers can affect a wide variety of both physical and psychological functions including heart rate, sleep, appetite, mood, and fear. Billions of neurotransmitter molecules work constantly to keep our brains functioning, managing everything from our breathing to our heartbeat to our learning and concentration levels."

Neurotransmitters send chemical messages between neurons. Mental illnesses, such as depression, can occur when this process does not work correctly. When this happens, you will see the signs, which often show up as the red flags listed above. If you notice these signs, it's time to take action, for yourself or on behalf of someone you love. Parents are the best advocates for their children, and the more seriously you take their mental health, the healthier they will live with their diagnoses.

Depression in teens can be a result of chemical changes in the brain due to stress or even hormonal changes. No matter how teenage depression occurs, it's important to get help restoring the brain's chemical balance. Prolonged depression can lead to self-destructive behaviors including risk-taking, cutting, self-harm, substance abuse, and even suicide.

Social Media Depression

It doesn't take a rocket scientist or a psychiatrist to see evidence that links mental illness in our young people to the increased use of social media in society.

I met a sixteen-year-old boy whom I referred back to the school counselor after he shared with me that he was harming himself. His arms and legs were all cut up and scraped and this was probably the worst evidence of self-harm I had ever seen — and I have seen a lot.

Under the guidance of his family physician, their first plan of action was to put him on antidepressants. I stayed in touch with this boy and the parents through the process and offered some other suggestions, too. As I chatted with this boy for some time, it sounded to me like his use of social media was having a negative impact on his mental health. He was spending untold hours online and felt he was missing out on all of the exciting things he saw other kids doing. I suggested a simple solution.

I told him to start weaning himself from social media, restricting himself to just an hour before he went to bed. When he went to bed, his parents took the phone for the night. After a few weeks, I suggested they give him some more rights and privileges and extend his time to thirty minutes in the morning and allow him ninety minutes at night. This practice of limiting social media would benefit all teens, depressed or not. I dare suggest it would benefit adults as well, huh?

With the parents seeking help, the boy acknowledging he needed help, the doctor finding a medication that worked, and the parents and the boy deciding together to limit his social media and online time and attend therapy, I am proud to say this young man has reported a significant improvement in his well-being.

After six months, I got a letter from his mother saying he was happier at school and was more involved in after-school activities. His interaction with his friends also improved.

Balance and boundaries. Reset the mind. Reset the boundaries. If our teens can't do it for themselves, then parents need to step up and take the phone away until their children can use their devices responsibly.

Treating Teen Depression

There are several things you can do that can immediately benefit yourself, or the teen in your life who needs help — and self-care is one of those things. If you find yourself feeling high-strung, quick-tempered, or dealing with extreme emotions, this is a clear sign that you are overloaded and need to slow down.

I have learned the benefit of self-care, and I practice self-care daily. I put this high on the list (along with counseling and medication) as to why I am the healthiest I have ever been. Hey, I don't want to scare you. This isn't some voodoo practice or some otherworldly routine. Self-care is as simple as putting yourself and your own needs first. Remember how flight attendants tell you to put on your own oxygen mask before you help others? Self-care is like that.

Medicating a child under the age of seventeen is risky, and I don't necessarily think it's a great idea. While medications can certainly help, they need to be part of an overall treatment plan. The last thing we want to do is add to the growing number of overmedicated children.

Most doctors are only given minutes to make a diagnosis and suggest a treatment plan, so the more information parents can give a doctor, the better. I suggest that parents keep a journal before a doctor visit, documenting the child's signs and symptoms. If the child is prescribed medication, the parent should note in that journal any positive or negative changes between check ups to help the doctor determine whether the medication is working properly. Detailed notes can go a long way in helping to make sure the doctor has all the information necessary to arrive at a proper diagnosis and will also serve as a progress report moving forward.

If you were to ask me what I think is more important, medication or counseling, I would say to get your child into therapy first. Therapy will teach your child how to cope better and process their emotions in a positive way. It will also arm your child with the problem-solving skills needed to face the challenges that come their way. Sometimes, medication alone is like putting a Band-Aid on a situation, but if coupled with therapy, the results can be life changing. As parents, we need to lose our egos, open our hearts, and set aside any preconceived notions about how we think things *should* go. News flash: We could be wrong. Just because you haven't experienced mental health issues or you have had misconceptions about the topic doesn't mean your child isn't struggling.

Parental Vigilance is Key: Monitor Screen Time

There are a few key things that we can do to help our teens. If you see that a child is isolated for any reason or is spending too much time online, it's time to take action. Schools should prohibit smartphone use until classes are over. This will require the support of the parents, who should understand that their kids are in school to learn. Snapchat can wait. Parents don't need to text their kids while they are in school. Connectivity and technology are here to stay, but sound parenting should be here to stay, too.

As parents, we need to become more aware and present in the lives of our children. We should be watching, monitoring, and teaching balance and boundaries. If this doesn't happen at home, you can expect a lot more trouble in the coming years. We must implement mandated offline time for our children. Offline from *all* devices.

I've met teens who deliberately lose or break their phones, just to end distressing messages or the pain of being stalked or cyber bullied. It is an extreme way to get away from the inherent stress of being connected at all times. Girls as young as ten are developing body issues because of the unrealistic expectations of beauty in pictures they are bombarded with on social media platforms. This is alarming and downright frightening to mental health professionals and school counselors.

Our young people pay attention to what their peers post and often get upset because they feel that their lives don't live up in comparison. They see the best version of their friends' lives; it's easy to appear glamorous and successful online.

A study conducted in 2017 by The Royal Society of Public Health asked 1,500 young people between eleven and twenty-five years of age to track their moods while using the five most popular social media sites. It suggested Snapchat and Instagram were the most likely to inspire feelings of inadequacy and anxiety. YouTube had the most positive influence.

Seventy percent said Instagram (owned by Facebook) made them feel worse about body image and half the fourteen to twenty-four-year-olds reported that Instagram and Facebook exacerbated feelings of anxiety. Two-thirds of the participants said Facebook made cyberbullying worse. Social media sites such as Snapchat, Instagram, Facebook, and others are doing their best to make these sites safer. In time, I think you'll see some changes — but also remember that our young people are given access to these platforms without having the emotional capacity and maturity to process what all this means.

These social media platforms have become a space for young people to build relationships, shape their identities, express themselves, and learn about people and the world around them. All of this is very much linked to their overall mental health.

Think about this for a second. Back in the day when cell phones first arrived, you never would have interrupted a face-to-face conversation to answer a call or respond to a text. Today, however, it seems the phone takes priority as soon as it rings or a notification comes through. Isn't that proof enough of how much of an addiction this has become?

If we don't change how we parent our children, we are going to see a greater increase in the need for mental health services for our youth. Our government doesn't have enough funding, nor do I think it has been a great priority for our government to make more resources available. Teen suicide will likely continue to increase without education and awareness.

And what about teens who express their opinions online about alternate views on sexuality or politics? You guessed it, they open themselves up to the same potential torrent of abuse on social media platforms that many adults experience every day. Cyberbullying is intense, and it is something that we as parents have never had to go through. Can you imagine what this onslaught of abuse might feel like to your child? It's a lot to deal with for adults, let alone a young person. It's no wonder they don't speak up. They don't know what to say or how to say it because they aren't exactly sure how they feel.

At school, bullying is limited to being in school, but cyberbullying invades a child within their own four walls — the safety of their bedroom. Many feel trapped; many feel they have no way to escape the abuse. I worry about teens who simply stop going out because of their addiction to online gaming or social media. They increase what harms them instead of boosting their self-esteem and benefiting their mental health by getting out and interacting with their peers. Many schools bring in mental health professionals, but many at-risk teens refuse to see them or even talk. It can be embarrassing to be called out of class, in front of everybody, to go see a mental health counselor whom they don't trust. Some parents prefer their children avoid talking to counselors; they don't want others knowing their family business. And many teens don't want to talk to someone they don't know or have any relationship with. The stigma is just too great.

Counseling isn't a quick fix scenario. It could take months to make any headway with a teen to enable them to conquer their online addiction, leave their bedrooms, and become more active socially. This process does not happen overnight. Why do you think this is? It's very simple when you realize that many of our teens prefer living in a fictional world — a world that can be detrimental to their physical and mental health. If we don't place limits on their time in that world, it will only become harder for them to face harsh realities in the real world when they become an adult with responsibilities.

Imagine sleeping with the Wi-Fi router unplugged to make sure your child isn't going online in the middle of the night. Some parents do that!

Even if you think your child doesn't have an issue with social media or excessive online time, the internet can still present dangers because it has become a conduit into the lives of friends and celebrities.

Who is raising your child? Who is most influential? I haven't even mentioned online predators and pedophiles who interact with kids on social media every day. Dr. Phil says that the most influential person in a child's life is that same-sex parent.

<u>What Parents Can Do:</u>

» Keep an eye on how much time children spend online and ensure it is not interfering with activities such as socializing, exercising, eating, and sleeping.

» Consider taking the smartphone and devices away during times such as mealtimes as well as an hour before bedtime. Do not let children charge devices in their rooms.

» Talk regularly with your teens about what they're doing online: what they choose to post, who their friends are, and how other people's posts affect their mood.

» If the smartphone is part of your account, you need to have access to passwords and regularly check content and pictures on the phone as well as social media accounts.

» Many social media accounts do not allow children under thirteen to have their own accounts. This is their policy, but many kids lie about their age. Parents, you are in the wrong if your child is under thirteen and has an account. Regardless of other kids having accounts before age thirteen, you need to follow the law and protect your child. You need to set an example and show your children they must follow rules.

» Encourage children to use the internet for educational and creative projects like research for homework or producing their own content. Encourage the use of positive, helpful, and inspirational websites.

» Teach your children that they're establishing their online identity every day not only by what they post, but also how they are represented in tagged pictures, posts, and messages.

You Matter

Did you know that nearly twenty million teens in the United States have parents with mental health issues?

If mental illness is in your family, you are at greater risk of developing mental illness yourself. This isn't meant to alarm you, but to awaken you to acknowledge and accept it. If you are suffering from signs of mental illness, seek help immediately. The sooner you recognize it and seek treatment, the sooner you will be on your path to healthy living.

If you think you might be at risk for depression, check out the questions on page 202 - Quiz. If any of these questions resonate with you, speak with a doctor. Ask questions.

CHAPTER 8

SELF-CARE

Self-Care

Take time to do what makes your soul happy.

You know how air flight attendants instruct you to put on your own oxygen mask first before helping others? This is the point behind the term self-care — a broad term for the things you do every day to be good to yourself. It's doing the necessary work so that your emotional reserves don't run dry. You can't pour from an empty pitcher. You can't spend from an empty bank account. You can't drive your car without gas. Makes sense, right?

Self-care is positive and productive — the polar opposite of self-destructive behaviors. Do not be fooled into believing that using alcohol or drugs, overeating, or compulsive risk-taking are in any way related to self-care. These are unhealthy coping mechanisms that many people believe will help them face challenging situations or emotional upsets. These behaviors might seem like a quick fix, but could lead to addiction and despair. Without exception, any perceived relief from these unhealthy actions will be temporary at best and the pain will remain.

On the upside, self-care is good for you in every aspect of your life — now and in the future. It benefits you in everything you do. Unhealthy coping mechanisms can and will destroy your life personally and professionally. It might not seem that way when you are young, but those things eventually catch up to you. By practicing self-care daily, you will begin to reap many benefits in your life. I am constantly amazed by the effect it has on my mood and my energy levels.

Benefits from Self-Care

1. Increased Productivity: Self-care is all about making sure that you do not overextend yourself. Learn to say "no" to what doesn't benefit you or to things that will cause you to spread yourself too thin. What matters to you the most? What is important and what is not? Relationships are give-and-take and need to be balanced. This isn't selfish. Slow down and remain in control. Remember this: Fast is slow and slow is fast. Take the time to do things right from the get-go so that you save time in the end. Arrive sooner and you

will be more relaxed. Paradoxically, you will achieve things faster and enjoy more abundance.

2. Better Health: There is evidence that most self-care activities activate your parasympathetic nervous system (PNS). This means that your body goes into a restful, rejuvenating mode, helping the body to fortify its immune system. Better self-care results in fewer illnesses.

3. Improved Self-Esteem: Taking the time to take care of yourself and meeting your own needs first sends positive messages to your subconscious. You are treating yourself like you matter, and you matter first. You have value to offer others, but you need to recognize that value. By practicing self-care, you are tapping into a well of deep personal value.

4. Heightened Self-Awareness: Practicing self-care teaches you to think about what really matters to you and what you enjoy doing — and puts you in in touch with passion and inspiration. This helps you to understand what really makes you tick. Sometimes, self-care can inspire you to make necessary changes that you might have overlooked if you weren't taking this time for yourself.

5. More to Give: Being good to yourself means that you will be better to others. Remember, this isn't about being selfish. Self-care gives you what you need so that you can give others kindness, compassion, and empathy, and be more present in everyday life.

We live in a world that can sometimes seem like complete insanity. The news is usually very negative. There are stories of shootings, natural disasters, and divisive political coverage that flood the airwaves. The repetitive twenty-four-hour news cycle only serves to amplify feelings of being overwhelmed. The world is in chaos. I can't allow myself to get caught up in all of this. I know that some triggers will affect my emotions and ultimately own my day, making it very difficult for me to do what I do best.

I'm not going to get weird and spiritual on you, but I am going to mention therapy, self-care, and what you can do that serves you and your close circle of family and friends.

Body and Mind

Body

For so many years, I neglected to take care of my body. I needed a wake-up call to make changes. Many of us take better care of our cars, homes, and pets than we take care of our bodies. Think about that.

For a very long time, I continued to eat the way I ate as an active teen and later a United States Marine. Food was my comfort and my refuge. I coped with life by eating, especially when I was on the road. After a grueling day of speaking, I'd reward myself (or so I thought) with a big, greasy cheeseburger or a nice, juicy steak and baked potato. Then I'd wash it all down with soda. Not just one soda, but two or three sodas. All that sugar!

Little by little, that caught up to me. I had warning signs too, but I never paid attention because they were just warnings. Ever notice that we usually don't change until we have to? Why is that? Change is hard. Change is growth and you are responsible. I let my body go — just let it go until I was forced to make a change or die.

You only get one body. That's it. Challenge it with daily exercise. Keep the body strong. Stretch and maintain flexibility and mobility. Put good stuff *in* your body and you'll get good results *from* your body.

Drugs and alcohol destroy your body and your mind. Self-medicating destroys any success you gain with therapy and medication prescribed by a medical professional.

Mind

The mind is our greatest asset, and yet we don't always fill it with good things. We waste our minds daily in so many ways — playing video games excessively, stalking social media, looking up stupid, irrelevant stuff on the internet and YouTube to pass the time. Don't get me wrong. In moderation, I think a little mental downtime is fine. But moderation doesn't seem to exist anymore.

Are violent video games desensitizing the minds of our youth? They certainly do not help. So many games, such as *Grand Theft Auto*, are not just desensitizing, but also dehumanizing. I played it once. After five minutes of game play, I felt like I needed to take a shower. I felt dirty and disgusted. Parents, make sure your children and teens are only playing age-appropriate video games. There are a lot of very young children playing violent video games online as well as interacting with strangers every day. I believe that moderation is key in all aspects of screen time and social media.

The mind is a powerful tool, and we should use it daily in a meaningful way. We don't always take opportunities to educate ourselves and expand our knowledge base.

Instead of gaming, overloading ourselves with dumb videos on YouTube, and being so concerned with what everyone is doing on social media, we can choose to use our smartphones to learn. Forget Snapchat for a minute and look up an answer to a question you might have. Think of a new question tomorrow and look that up. Can you imagine what you will know in a year? The smartphone can be your own personal library of information.

We don't need to be in a classroom to learn about what inspires and excites us. What excites you? What motivates you? Is it computer technology? Is it learning to cook healthy meals? Is it being the best athlete you can be and finding drills that work for you? Is it getting into the best college? What about designing a website and learning WordPress, HTML, or SEO? How about making your own videos and learning how to create and edit your own Vlogs for YouTube and Instagram?

I ask these questions because we need to think and act deliberately about the direction of our lives. Many of you will go to college and some of you will be entrepreneurs. Make the most of your opportunities and learn all you can. Employers today are more concerned about your experiences, what you know, and what you have done. There is reduced emphasis on whether or not you went to a fancy, expensive school. Take it upon yourself to grow and gain as much knowledge every day as possible. Get ahead. Use the internet to benefit and challenge your mind.

Cognitive-Behavioral Therapy (CBT)

For those young people who choose to seek professional help, this might begin with a school mental health counselor, who might potentially make a recommendation for outside therapy and ongoing counseling.

Psychology Today defines cognitive-behavioral therapy as "a form of psychotherapy that treats problems and boosts happiness by modifying dysfunctional emotions, behaviors, and thoughts. CBT focuses on solutions, encouraging patients to challenge distorted cognitions and change destructive patterns of behavior."

CBT encompasses many forms of treatment that can give a patient concrete steps they can take to interrupt negative thoughts and behaviors. It has also been used to treat people with phobias and fears, such as fear of flying on an airplane. CBT is a very practical method of treatment that focuses more on behavior and less on discussing the past. CBT has long been the foundation of my self-care, and it has done wonders for me. It can do the same for yourself and/or your teen.

CBT is my favorite type of counseling and has been a blessing in my life since my spinal cord fusion and my diabetes scare; CBT helped me rekindle my passion and reinvent my career.

Medication

When most teens are treated by a medical professional for emotional or mental health matters, they are usually prescribed an antidepressant. This is a start, but it's not always the answer. Developing a treatment plan for a teen isn't like plugging in a formula and waiting for the process to spit out an answer. It's not that simple.

You might argue that doctors are overmedicating our kids today. I don't disagree, but this is more a parenting problem than the doctor's fault. Advocacy on the part of the parent and child is the best answer for long-term benefits. Again, doctors have limited time to make a diagnosis, prescribe medication, or create treatment plans, and this becomes more difficult when information is incomplete. Diagnosing teens is something that many general practitioners don't feel comfortable doing, in large part because of the many physical and emotional changes teens go through. Thus, I reiterate — a detailed journal is vital.

Earlier, I mentioned the importance of keeping a journal noting the results and effects of prescribed medications. It is very important to track behavior and any adverse effects, so a doctor can determine what works and what does not. You can then go back to the doctor with the information they need to chart a more thorough course of action.

In the event your teen experiences side effects from medication or possibly has suicidal thoughts, contact your physician right away and ask what they recommend regarding medication until your teen can be seen professionally. Trust the doctor's advice. If you need to take action immediately, call 911 or take your child to the emergency room without hesitation.

It's imperative that parents are involved in this process. If you do not struggle with mental illness, you must learn to recognize the signs. You need to be aware of how mental illness might affect your child, while making sure that you refrain from judging or make your child feel "less than." Your support and encouragement will make things much easier for both of you. You can make a big difference in how your child responds to professional help, medication, counseling, and/or therapy. Please take this seriously. This is in the best interest of your child.

Mindfulness

My favorite definition of mindfulness comes from an excellent website called Mindful (midful.org):

"Mindfulness suggests that the mind is fully attending to what's happening in the here and the now, to what you're doing, to the space you're moving through."

Most of us let our minds wander and we have difficulty paying attention to what goes on around us. Mindfulness can help us connect with our thoughts, our bodies, and other people. Being completely present with our thoughts and our actions can help all of us feel less anxious and overwhelmed.

To me, mindfulness is a short practice that restores your awareness of your breath and your body, bringing you back to being centered — so you feel calmer and more at ease in your emotions, feelings, and thoughts.

The first step in mindfulness is to stop what you are doing, just pause. If you are in a classroom, give yourself permission to take a moment, put the pen down, and just stop. Breathe. Allow yourself a minute or two just to *be*.

Take a deep breath. Pay attention to the inhale. Pay attention to the exhale. Breathe without forcing or changing your breath pattern — four seconds on the inhale and four seconds on the exhale. This helps you connect with how you feel, and soon your breathing will begin to feel more natural, and your heart rate will slow down. Bring your breath into your belly — your inner core — and become aware of how your belly expands and contracts. This type of breathing practice calms and centers your body and mind.

The point is that you have allowed yourself to stop whatever you were doing in order to be present. *That* is being mindful.

Are you stressed? Are you in crisis? Are you dizzy? Are you lightheaded? Do you feel the urge to race out and finish whatever you were doing, or do you feel the urge to stay put for a second? Are you feeling connected or disconnected to your body? The objective here is to achieve a connection between your breathing and how you are feeling and stay present in the moment.

It's really important to acknowledge where your mind goes during this process. It is important to allow different thoughts and sensations to surface. By being mindful, you will start to settle down and recognize that you have more control over your thoughts and emotions than you might have previously considered.

I make mindfulness practice a part of my day, and I highly recommend that you do the same.

Meditation

Life happens, and our emotions are often a product of what is going on around us and within us. Much of this is beyond our control. However, you can choose to accept that you are not a victim of what happens around you and you can choose to be a victor. A simple pattern shift of your thinking can help you take responsibility for your mind and thoughts — and change them for the better. You can also replace your expectations for appreciation as well as change your mindset.

> *"Growth means change and change involves risk, stepping from the known to the unknown."*
>
> - GEORGE SHINN

According to Buddhism, meditation is the most important thing you can do. Meditation is being mindful of what you need for yourself. During meditation, you are mindful of where your thoughts are and where you want them to be. You're also being mindful of your emotions, your emotional bank account. That is why we meditate: to become aware of what we need for our mental well-being.

Maybe you need to get more clarity, reduce stress and anxiety, find more energy for optimal performance, and/or gain insight and awareness through the observation of your own mind and emotions, whatever it is you need. Through meditation, you can tap into the power of the mind and make necessary changes.

Without getting too spiritual, I want to share with you my experiences with mindfulness and meditation.

Years ago, I became demanding regarding how the room was set up when I was speaking to an audience. I didn't like myself, or the way I was feeling. I knew I needed to revisit my thinking and make some changes. This was about the same time as my life crisis, depression, raging diabetes, and spinal cord fusion. I decided to commit to yoga and a morning routine. Meditation, breathing, and being mindful were all a part of my daily routine.

I contribute my current health to my morning practice of self-care, meditation, mindfulness, yoga, and breathing.

So, what I needed and what I continue to need is to transform my mind through meditation. Sometimes, I take a quick time-out in the middle of my day and center myself, meditate and breathe. I call it regrouping.

I have learned to engage in my own morning routine of meditation, breathing, mindfulness, and affirmations. This has become a habit and the daily practice has made me more present, energized, positive, and engaged. By disciplining myself and engaging in mindfulness and meditation, I have found clarity and a depth of peace and calmness with a clearer sense of my mind. This practice has really shaped me into a better person: more engaged, more passionate, and stronger. I have a better understanding of who I am and how I am. I am very grateful this practice has given me a new understanding of life.

Breathing

One secret in my journey has been learning to breathe properly. These methods have been a life-changer and have significantly reduced my anxiety and depression. Breathing has also proven to be the fastest way for me to calm down.

This is a yoga type of breathing I practice called *pranayama*, which is the regulation of the breath through certain techniques and exercises. These maneuvers quickly increase energy, release stress, and can improve mental clarity as well as physical health.

Pranayama is the control of *prana*, or the breath, and the techniques rely on breathing through the nostrils. The ancient sages of India realized that these breathing practices made a major difference in their well-being. Performed correctly, pranayama brings harmony to the body, mind, and spirit — strengthening all of these components and unifying them as a whole.

Pranayama goes a step further than simple awareness of the breath. It uses specific rhythms and techniques to provide numerous benefits on mental, emotional, and physical levels. Personally, I've experienced a sense of calmness; I find this practice helpful in achieving mindfulness.

The benefits of pranayama that I have noticed:

» Calmness in my mind
» Less worry and less anxiety, especially after I practice breathing
» Focus and clarity in what I am doing
» Gratitude coupled with more energy
» Reduced illness
» Feeling recharged and ready

Renowned author and entrepreneur Anthony Robbins has long considered proper breathing techniques to be instrumental in changing a person's mental state, thereby opening them up to real and lasting change. Thousands of people have benefitted from his self-help and self-actualization programs.

This type of breathing is also connected to emotions. Do you notice when you are angry your breathing gets deeper, faster, and more deliberate? When I am calm, my breathing is steady and even.

While we aren't always successful in controlling our emotions, we can learn to control our breath. Doing so can help us realize what we are feeling and what we need to change or focus on. If we understand the rhythm of our breath, we have a better chance to control our thoughts. We can win over any negative emotions like anger, jealousy, or greed, and we are able to smile more from our heart. Given how difficult it is to control emotions, using specific yogic breathing techniques to transform overpowering and negative emotions becomes a powerful tool for enhancing well-being and inner peace.

As I like to say, "Inhale peace — exhale love." Or when I am really struggling, "Inhale – I know I am inhaling. Exhale – I know I am exhaling." Stay focused on the breathing.

Time-Outs

My therapist actually wants me to take every fourth day off as a time-out day. Remember the anger you felt as a child when you were sent to time-out? It's different as an adult, especially when under orders from a mental health professional. It's amazing, and I have been tempted to use this to my advantage (don't tell my therapist) when it suits me.

"Ah, no, honey! I can't run those errands today, because today is my scheduled time-out day."

Yeah, that doesn't work, but you get the point.

Every fourth day, my therapist wants me to pay extra attention to self-care. That could mean that I don't need to be in the office from eight in the morning to seven at night. Instead, I can finish a work task at home and then go golfing... and not feel bad about it. Imagine if you made time-outs part of your routine in order to practice mindfulness, meditation, and breathing as part of your self-care plan? Wouldn't this be incredible? Remember, you can't pour from an empty pitcher. Put the oxygen mask on yourself first before you attempt to help others.

In my growth as a man who lives with mental illness, this has changed my life in ways I can't even begin to explain. It's now a daily part of my self-care plan and something I do before I arrive for any speaking engagement. I take a time-out before I have to be present and engaged. I've noticed an incredible difference in my activities and the products of my work.

The Power of Gratitude

Learn to replace your expectations with appreciation. I say "thank you" at least twenty-five times a day. Whether I am experiencing something good or bad, everything we go through is a learning experience that contributes to our personal growth. We are shaped by every challenge and obstacle as much as we are shaped by every victory and success — so I say "thank you" to everything that comes my way. Imagine if you started doing this? Find appreciation in everything, good and bad, and let this new appreciation replace your expectations. This is a life-changer when practiced regularly.

Jeff's Daily Self-Care Practice

My friend Hal Elrod endorsed my Amazon bestseller, *BOOM! One Word to Instantly Inspire Action, Deliver Rewards, and Positively Affect Your Life Every Day!*

Hal's book, *The Miracle Morning*, is a blessing to millions of people. As a matter of fact, it's even been turned into a movie. I highly recommend you read his book and understand his acronym, SAVERS, which outlines six actions to take every morning.

SAVERS stands for Silence, Affirmations, Visualization, Exercise, Reading, and Scribing (writing).

Here is how I apply the six actions to my daily self-care:

Silence

> *"Silence is a source of great strength."*
>
> - LAO TZU

At first, I struggled with this. Silence was very difficult for me, but before long I came to enjoy it. No, this doesn't mean being quiet while checking social media, but your smartphone *can* come in handy in this case. There are several awesome apps out there to help you with your quiet time, including *Calm*, *Headspace*, *10% Happier*, and *Zen*. Even Oprah Winfrey and Deepak Chopra have a useful app called *Oprah & Deepak's Meditation Experience.* These are all great apps that help with mindfulness, meditation, and breathing. Like searching for the perfect pair of running shoes, you need to try them on for size.

Depending on the day, where I am, and what I need, I spend anywhere from five to thirty minutes in quiet time. I do this at least once a day, but sometimes it's three to five times a day. This helps me calm my mind, lower my anxiety, and start my day from a position of serenity and purpose.

Because I am not rushed, I use this time to be aware of the nuances in my senses and slow my breathing. I reduce my anxiety level in half within about three minutes. Running on a high level of anxiety isn't healthy and it certainly isn't productive. It's simply not where I want to be.

Let's talk about you. On a scale of one to ten with one being low anxiety and ten being really high, where are you day-to-day, week-to-week, and month-to-month? On average, where would you say you are? I am usually at a five to seven, but I want to be between two to four; I want to be in control and aware. This way, if something does trigger an unhealthy emotion, my anxiety level might rise from a four to six, but at that level, I am still capable of making good decisions and coping with anything. If I spike up to a seven or nine, I need a time-out — and sometimes I can't take a time-out. I always want to be in control of my emotions rather than allowing something to trigger my feelings resulting in hours or days of recovery. This daily practice keeps me in control (most of the time). Therapy and counseling has taught me coping skills and problem-solving skills when my emotions have won and I am triggered. I'm doing very well, and I contribute my success to doing the work.

I find that a lot of young people today are above level five in regards to anxiety.

I even meet teens who report anxiety levels over ten and I'm like, "Dude, I didn't even give you that as an option."

They're like, "Yeah, well I'm there."

That is really concerning to me. As a teen, if you are living with anxiety above a level seven, it's not good overall or in the long run.

Silence is really important first thing in the morning. If you feel your anxiety levels going up during the day, find a quiet spot and take a few minutes. Being aware is key. You know where you are emotionally. You know where you are with stress and anxiety. If your level is too high, then take the time to bring yourself back down.

Affirmations

Affirmations are about boosting your self-confidence and making statements to reaffirm what you need or what you already know in the event self-doubt shows up. They are self-talk reminders to help you focus on positivity and growth. Here are affirmations I used after my return from my near-death experience in 2015–2016 from spinal cord fusion, depression, and my diabetes scare. I'm happy to share with you. These helped me rebuild my life, my career, my self-esteem, and myself.

Use these affirmations as a template to create your own:

1 Business Affirmation

I have an awesome career with amazing opportunity for growth. I have the perfect job. I am a life-changer and a difference-maker. The more I give of myself, the more business I create. My heart brings peace to the world. My voice gives hope and motivation to my audience. I am meant to speak to teens and families. I change lives and big things are coming my way.

2 Personal Affirmation

I am healthy and happy. My mind is calm. I am relaxed in every situation. I control my emotions. Nobody has power over my thoughts and feelings. I am above all outside influences. My thoughts are under my control. I radiate love and happiness. I am surrounded by an abundance of loving, supportive, and kind people. I am living in the house of my dreams. I have great and loving relationship with my wife, Janet.

3 Health Affirmation

My body is a temple. My body is healthy and functioning in a very positive way. I make great choices for energy and health by the foods I eat. I eat to live. I do not live to eat. I have an abundance of energy. My body improves daily.

4 Financial Affirmation

I am a moneymaking machine. Money is created through my energy and my heart. Wealth pours in all around me. I sail on the river of wealth. Each day, I get wealthier and wealthier. The money I earn is the result of the value I give to my clients. I give incredible value and I am worth the money I charge.

⑥ Spiritual Affirmation

God is my almighty father. Everything I do is through His grace. God works through my heart to give love and energy to the world. God says life is not perfect nor is perfection real. God gives me joy. God gives me love. God gave his only Son to sacrifice His life and die on the cross for all our sins. God is within me and strengthens me in everything I do.

Affirmations are powerful phrases that can bolster self-esteem. They pick us up when we feel down and keep us on the right path. I print them on index cards and keep them in the bathroom, and when I get ready for the day, I take a few minutes and do what I need to do. I face my own reflection in the mirror and I'm honest with myself.

I always say, if you don't like the reflection in the mirror, it's not the mirror's fault.

Don't save your affirmations just for the bathroom. Put them on your smartphone. Break them out before a game, a test, a date, or a job interview. Go in to any situation with confidence.

Visualization

Simply put, I close my eyes and visualize my success. My day is up to me. I will not let my emotions and thoughts own me or determine my outcome.

Before I do anything, I spend time visualizing a positive conclusion to the day. I see myself winning. I own my success. I visualize great things happening, playing out in my mind's eye.

Picture yourself accomplishing what you set out to accomplish. Before a game or a test, see yourself on the other side with a great result. Imagine that game-winning base hit. See yourself acing that test. Imagine owning all aspects of the day in front of you. Visualize the outcome you want. Positive thoughts equal a positive outcome. If you can see it and believe it, you have a better chance of achieving it.

Exercise

Activate your endorphins and you will improve your mood. Motion impacts emotion. Get moving —whether it's a walk, a workout in the gym, boot camp, yoga, or spinning. Aim for at least thirty minutes of solid exercise every day. Stretch. Make sure you stay limber and have good mobility. Burn off the toxins in your body. Get the blood flowing. Sweat. Release that stress. Exercise, along with proper nutrition and hydration, is key.

Reading

We are always learning, or at least we should be. Don't let the mind go to waste. Did you know that the average person reads less than ten percent of one book per year? We can't even squeeze in a whole book anymore? Let this sink in: if you read for only fifteen minutes per day, you will have read eighteen books in just one year. Does that sound as amazing to you as it does to me?

Reading can also improve your overall mental health. In November of 2010, the University of Liverpool published the results of a study entitled: An Investigation into the Therapeutic Benefits of Reading in Relation to Depression and Well-Being. The study found that group "... [r]eading helped patients suffering from depression in terms of: their social well-being, by increasing personal confidence and reducing social isolation; their mental well-being, by improving powers of concentration and fostering an interest in new learning or new ways of understanding; their emotional and psychological well-being, by increasing self-awareness and enhancing the ability to articulate profound issues of self and being."

Maybe I should join my wife's Book Club?

Scribing
Scribing is just a fancy word for writing. Whether I am writing a new book, a blog, or journaling, I take my time. Writing slows down your brain, allows you to process your thoughts, and helps you think more clearly. It's OK to write down your deepest thoughts and feelings.

You will be amazed what happens when you write down a plan of action for the day, week, and month. Writing a to-do list gives you clarity and purpose. Scribing gives you a roadmap as well as a record of where you have been.

Self-Care Checkup

If you are between age thirteen and twenty-four, this can be a very unsettling time in your life — but you have the power and the control to take action. Life is going to throw some challenges your way, but I just gave you some ideas to empower you to own your emotions, take control of your thoughts and feelings, and practice self-care. If you step out in faith and begin to implement these principles, you will be the most successful person you are capable of being. I have faith in you.

Get out some paper and a pencil or pen. Take some time to answer the following questions:

 What does self-care mean to you?

2. What did you learn about self-care that you can implement immediately in your life?

3. What are three things you are going to start doing to practice self-care and commit to?

In every talk I give, I ask this question: How many of you would admit that you're probably a little lazy? Every hand goes up.

Stop being lazy and choose to be intelligent and awesome. You were not born to be average. You choose to be average. You are not a victim. You choose to be a victim. Choose to live healthy, be educated, smart, kind, caring, strong, present, and engaged. Choose to take back your life and own it regardless of situations, circumstances, and anything else that is taking you away from you being your best.

Giving Permission

Because I am self-employed, one of the biggest issues I have is that I always have to be connected and I am always working. I need to be careful because of my own mental health issues. I have always had a nagging fear that if I am not busy working, others are working harder than I am, and I will fail in my own business. It doesn't matter how successful I have become over decades in my business. One slip-up and someone else will outwork me, and failure is not an option.

Do you see how unreasonable and unsustainable this is?

After all these years, I have finally come to realize that it's not so much about working *harder* as it is about working *smarter*. It's not about working fifteen-hour days, but rather maximizing my time and being productive in the work I am doing. It's about time management.

I've learned that I need to give myself permission to take time off to focus on my health, my attitude, my emotions, and my overall well-being. If I don't do that, I can become quick-tempered and not so much fun to be around. I don't like this about myself, and it's not fair to those I love and to those who love me.

Permission granted. I say to myself that this time off is crucial to my personal growth. It makes me stronger and allows me to be present and engaged when I return to my work. My work is intense — and if I am not present and engaged, I am cheating my clients. I never want to cheat a client and I always want to be authentic. This authenticity allows me to better serve those who trust in me.

Where do you need to give yourself permission?

This permission is necessary for all young people. Scratch that. I think this is useful for almost everybody. Give yourself permission to take time off from being "on" all the time. Take time off from your smartphone. Take time off from social media and the internet.

Do what I do. Start with Sundays. I call it Smartphone-Free Sunday. Try it, and then stop taking your phone to bed with you. Leave it downstairs in the kitchen. Turn it off and let it charge in another room. Enjoy your peace and quiet within your own four walls.

There's your challenge. Give yourself permission to try it. I bet you'll enjoy it as much as I do.

Self-Care has changed
Jeff's life. Yoga, Breathing,
Meditation.

CHAPTER 9

A WORD ABOUT LOSS AND GRIEVING

The Five Stages of Grief

> *"Grief is the price we pay for love."*
> — QUEEN ELIZABETH II

You've probably heard about the stages of grief. You need to be sure to acknowledge them. You owe it to yourself to get through them; you owe it to yourself to reach the point of acceptance.

1 **Denial and Isolation: This can't be Real!**

Being in denial doesn't mean you don't care. After a student was informed her father had been killed in a car accident, we couldn't find her. Eventually we discovered her working on the homecoming float. I was with a good friend of hers and a counselor. When we asked her if she was OK, she replied, "Yeah, we have to get this float done." She was in denial; she wasn't ready to face the pain. She was numb. She was in shock. She was trying to occupy her mind so she didn't have to accept the loss. This is common at first.

2 **Anger and Blame: It's not Fair!**

Another common stage is being angry and placing blame. This can happen when we feel helpless and powerless over a loss. We can feel abandoned, and we might even be angry with God or a higher power. Or maybe we blame the doctors, focusing our anger on them. Then we are angry at life in general.

3 **Bargaining: If Only…**

This stage of grief is about incessantly thinking about what could have been done to prevent the death or loss. Some people even become obsessed with things they could have done differently to save the person's life. This stage needs to be dealt with because if it isn't dealt with properly, the person may live a life with intense feelings of guilt or anger that interfere with the healing process.

4 **Depression: They're really gone…**

This stage is where we begin to realize and feel the true extent of the death or loss. This usually happens about a week or two after the services and funeral, and after people have gone back to normal activity and their everyday lives. Common signs of depression in this stage of grieving include self-pity, trouble sleeping, poor appetite, fatigue, lack of energy, and crying spells. We may also feel lonely, isolated, empty, lost, and/or anxious. To combat this, we need to try and get back into normal habits, routines, and everyday life as quickly as possible so this stage doesn't last too long.

Acceptance: OK, that happened.
This is the stage we work toward — acceptance. Grieving has no timetable and nobody should ever tell you how long the process takes because it is different for each person.

In time, we come to terms with all the emotions and feelings we experience when death or loss happens. And once we do, we can begin to heal.

Throughout our lives, it's possible to return to some of the earlier stages of grief, such as depression or anger. There are no rules or time limits to the grieving process. Everyone heals differently. Some people don't experience all five stages of grief and those who do might go through them in a different order. Don't ever let anyone tell you that you should "be over it by now"; grief has no set schedule. It's all personal, but it's important you are aware of the stages and process it all.

In my 2017 book, *BOOM! One Word to Instantly Inspire Action, Deliver Rewards, and Positively Affect Your Life Every Day*, I lay out a plan for folks to take responsibility for the direction of their lives, while celebrating victories along the way. Loss can be a stumbling block for many of us, and I felt compelled to share my thoughts about it.

The following comes from *BOOM!* I have included it here because we all experience loss in our lives:

Dealing with Loss

We are all going to die. The sooner we accept this fact, the sooner we really start to live.

Loss happens. It's a part of life, and that's something we need to understand. Whether we love somebody or something, we must accept the fact that nothing is forever — and that is why we should cherish the special moments that we experience in our lives. The reality that I really want to stress here is that everything is temporary. We are not on this planet for a long time, and when we lose someone, we realize how short time is.

The way you spell love is T-I-M-E, so really embrace the time you have with people — with things — with experiences. Life is made up of moments within events, and it's the moments we remember and cherish.

Sometimes it seems like we can't move on from our loss, but the surest way through this is to allow the grieving process to do its work. When we experience a loss, it's kind of like we have put all our eggs into one basket, and we are left with questions like, "What do I do now?" or "How can I possibly go on?"

Does loss hurt? Yes absolutely — and it's going to hurt forever.

There is also a lot of help available through therapy and counseling to help you move forward, but the way I really look at is that this is the circle of life. The Collins Dictionary defines the circle of life as "nature's way of taking and giving back life to earth. It symbolizes the universe being sacred and divine. It represents the infinite nature of energy, meaning if something dies it gives new life to another."

Whether it's a relationship that ends, you suffer the loss of a loved one or you find yourself out of a job — you have got to embrace opportunities for future growth. I don't think it's fair to assume that everything is permanent.

Always remember:

> *It's going to be OK.*

Life can be tough
but so are you!

Jeff Yalden

BE INFLUENTIAL... CHANGE THE WORLD!

Never lose hope. Keep believing.
Don't ever give up on yourself.

CHAPTER 10

TEEN SUICIDE

Suicidal Ideation

> *See Something; Say Something.*
> *Know Something; Do Something.*

Suicidal ideation is more commonly known as thinking about suicide. These thoughts can range from considering making that forever decision to mapping out a detailed plan for suicide.

Just because a teen is thinking about suicide does not mean that they will carry out the act. Thoughts of suicide are common. The majority does not follow up on these thoughts, but this does not mean they shouldn't be taken seriously. Without exception, all red flags are to be taken seriously and addressed immediately.

Some young people who attempt suicide don't intend to succeed. These are cries for help, and the plan is for the attempt to fail, but this could be a fatal miscalculation. Others meticulously plan every detail of the suicide, and they carry out their heartbreaking plan to the letter.

Facts about Suicidal Ideation

The American Foundation for Suicide Prevention provides some key points about suicidal ideation. You can find them at www.afsp.org.

You can also call The National Suicide Prevention Hotline toll-free at 800-273-8255, or you can text the Crisis Text Line by texting GO to 741741 to chat with a trained Crisis Counselor 24/7.

Here are some key points regarding suicide:

» Suicidal thoughts don't necessarily mean a suicide attempt is coming, but don't ignore the severity of the issue. These thoughts need to be addressed, especially if the thoughts are about harming oneself or others. Take these thoughts seriously and get help immediately.

» The idea that suicide rates are highest during the holidays is just a myth. Actually, in America, suicide rates are highest during the months of February through May.

» Nearly all completed suicides are among individuals with mental illness — depression.

» Suicide is rarely the result of one thing. However, one thing can certainly be the straw that breaks the camel's back.

- » The rate of suicide is highest in middle age men ages thirty-five to fifty (white men in particular). The research on this age group suggests these men faced trauma, but never dealt with it. That's why it's even more important that we work with our youth and encourage them to open up and share. It's OK to ask for HELP.
- » People with a family history of mental illness are more likely to have suicidal thoughts.
- » In America, suicides outnumber homicides by almost two-to-one.

Suicidal thoughts are preventable and there is plenty of help available.

Remember that young lady who told me she didn't reach out for help because "nobody asked her"? Help can't be given if nobody knows help is needed. Parents and teens, you are responsible for asking for help. The stigma starts with shame and that prevents many people for asking for help and reaching out. The only shame one should feel is in not asking for help. In my opinion, it is the strong people who have the courage to ask for help and not succumb to shame.

Causes of Suicidal Thoughts

Teens begin to think about suicide when they feel that they can no longer cope with overwhelming situations. The solutions to these problems seem so far out of reach that the teen can't move on. The desire for suicide can occur when the two factors of "I'm alone" and "I'm a burden" become too painful over a period of time.

When the teen's mental state is extremely heightened, suicide may seem to be their only option. Experts believe there may be a genetic factor associated with a higher risk of suicide. People with suicidal thoughts or those who have taken their own lives tend to have a family history of suicide or suicidal thoughts. There are also many psychiatric conditions that can lead to suicidal ideation.

<u>Psychiatric Factors Linked to a Higher Risk of Suicidal Ideation:</u>

- » Adjustment disorder
- » Anorexia nervosa
- » Bipolar disorder
- » Body dysmorphic disorder
- » Borderline personality disorder
- » Dissociative identity disorder
- » Gender dysphoria (gender identity disorder)
- » Major depressive disorder
- » Panic disorder
- » PTSD
- » Schizophrenia
- » Social anxiety disorder
- » Substance abuse

Suicidal Thoughts Triggered by Another Suicide

One person's suicide can have an impact on another's suicidal thoughts or their behaviors, especially among teenagers. Suicide can be contagious. A teenager does not have to personally know another teen who died by suicide to start having thoughts of suicide or attempting to end their own life.

When anybody dies, particularly a young person, the deceased is described in the media and social media in glowing, romantic terms. Often the deceased is described as beautiful, kind, and a good friend.

This is common when any child dies, but it can be very dangerous when the cause of death is suicide. Other teens are vulnerable, and they hear and read about how wonderful the deceased was. They want their loved ones to feel the same way about them, too.

You Are not Alone

You are not alone. Many of us have considered ending our lives. I know I did. I have a few times.

As a matter of fact, my therapist says she was concerned in 2016 that I was going to end my life. I don't think I was there, but she thought I was. Regardless, I was in bad shape, but I knew it was temporary and I was fighting to wake-up and get moving every day. I did the work.

You are not alone in this journey. If you are willing to do the work, I promise you'll come out of it a better person and very thankful you never made that forever decision.

I am willing to bet that a person close to you has thought about suicide — and it could be the person you least expect.

Here is what you need to know: Feeling suicidal isn't a flaw in one's character. It doesn't mean you are weak, different, crazy, or abnormal. It just means that you have more pain in your heart than you can deal with at the moment. This pain overwhelms you, and it feels like it won't go away. Reacting negatively is not going to help at all. Stop. Breathe. Take a time-out. Find a friend, or better yet, a trusted adult. Tell them how you are feeling. It might be hard to understand how this can help, but I beg you to trust me on this.

With time and support, you can overcome these seemingly overwhelming thoughts, feelings, and emotions. I promise. With just a little patience in the process, these mountains will become molehills, and your pain — along with the suicidal thoughts — will pass. I promise, my friend.

People from all walks of life experience suicidal thoughts. I have had them. Some of the most successful, most admired, and most prominent people have been where you are. Your friends, teachers, family, and others you know have probably had similar thoughts.

There Is Hope

Be patient and trust in the process.

Depression can be treated and hope can be restored. No matter the severity of the situation, time is your best friend. Time to breathe.

Time to practice self-care. Time to realize that you are loved and that people care about you deeply and unconditionally. What you are going through, whether you believe it or not, is temporary. I know it doesn't seem like it and you might be thinking, "Jeff, you don't understand!" I get that, but I can assure you that most of us have gone through painful moments in our lives where we felt the same way. Trust in the process. Trust in your people. Talk to them. As much as you think others don't understand, I know they do and they want to listen and help you through this. You just have to commit to one day at a time or even just one minute at a time. It will be OK. Just breathe and be willing to do the work.

It takes moral and physical courage to step back and do the right thing in these moments. Be selfish in these dark days. Dig deep into your well of inner strength to face this situation. You can do this. Figure out what you need to do for you in order to get better. Don't quit. The action of taking your life is a forever decision whereas what you are feeling and what you are going through is temporary. I promise.

I was suicidal in 1987 while in high school. Then again in 1992. I remember those days all too well. I remember them vividly. The pain, the numbness, justifying why I should die, thinking that ending my life would be doing everyone a favor. I don't exactly know why I didn't follow through with it. I remember being open and honest; I remember asking for help. I never felt ashamed. I'm proud of myself for that, and I am proud that I continue to see a counselor and take medication. I am proud that instead of being ashamed, I have embraced it.

Before I checked into the hospital in 1992, I talked to my grandmother, Mickey, three to four times a day on the phone. I shared my feelings with her and she didn't judge me. She listened. She told me to make it to the next meal.

I'd call her after breakfast and she would say, "Jeff, just make it to lunch. Don't do anything harmful and don't think too far ahead."

After dinner, she'd say, "Jeff, just make it to breakfast. It will be OK."

I vividly remember those words, those conversations, and where I was every time I called her. (On the payphone in the Marine barracks of Camp LeJeune, NC.) Perhaps it is because of Mickey that I am alive today.

Shortly after this time period, I met a young lady named Melissa who stole my heart. After a time, we broke up and split, but maybe meeting her and enjoying the relationship was the impetus I needed to get my mind off suicidal thoughts.

I credit my life today to Mickey and Melissa. My M&Ms.

I want you to know you are not alone. I want you to know you can overcome this and go on to do great things with your life. Because of my experiences, I discovered a job I love: working with young people, parents, educators, and mental health professionals to help everyone overcome life's struggles. I am truly grateful I get to share my story and help others. All this gratitude springs from the pain I suffered. The agony

I went through fuels my desire and provides me with a heart big enough to make a difference.

Where you are in life and the pain you feel in your heart might be because there is something for you on the other side. I believe that this pain will shape you and teach you and give you an opportunity you can't even imagine right now.

I encourage you to follow those words from my grandmother. Just make it to the next meal. After that, make it to the next one.

Suicide Is Not the Only Option

In a moment of crisis, it seems like your pain and unhappiness will never end and that suicide is the answer to everything. It is important to realize that most crises are temporary. You will find a solution, your feelings will change, and positive events will occur. Remember: suicide is a permanent action to a temporary problem. You need the time to breathe.

Suicide may seem like the only option, but it's not. There are other solutions that exist. Because you are so overwhelmed, you are not able to see them right now. You are overcome with emotions that can and will distort your thoughts and your circular thinking makes it almost impossible to see a way out of your problems.

Stop. Breathe. It's OK to feel. Regroup. Right now, these are only thoughts. Maybe in a couple of minutes, an hour or two — or even tomorrow — you will think to yourself, "OK, these are not healthy thoughts and I need to talk to someone." This is a great place to start.

Who can offer support? Who do you know? A teacher? A coach? Friends? What about your parents? If it makes you feel more comfortable, you can call any of the numbers listed in the back of this book. Do something. *Do something immediately.*

It's extremely important that you get to a therapist, counselor, friend, or loved one who can help you to see solutions that otherwise may not be apparent to you at the moment. Please give these people a chance. If anything, they will help you have a time-out and regroup.

If you are the friend of someone in a bad place and you see signs, you have a responsibility to do the right thing for your friend. Make the right decision and tell someone and/or bring this person to the right people. *Do not leave them alone.*

See something; say something. Know something; do something.

I know for me that when I get overwhelmed (yes, I still do), I take a time-out. I give myself space, and I always ask the question, "How can I fix this?" I want to know what fundamentally I can do in the here and the now to give space to the overwhelming emotions I am feeling. My friend, I am not writing this book from years of research and doctorate classes. I am writing this book because I did the work for myself first, and then

I spent years researching and learning. To me, this is worth more than a doctorate degree. I'm writing this because I care, and I want you to know you are not alone.

Remember this:

- » Your thoughts, feelings, and emotions are not fixed. They are fluid — they change day-to- day, week-to-week, month-to-month. How you feel today will not be the same as how you felt yesterday or how you will feel tomorrow or next week.
- » Taking your life would create grief and anguish in the lives of your friends and loved ones. You'd leave so many pieces that they would try to pick up for the rest of their lives. People love you. They need you. You matter.
- » There are many things you can still accomplish in your life. This is temporary, like the wind and the weather.
- » Life is beautiful when you get to the fundamentals. You would lose out on the sights, sounds, tastes, smells, and touches yet to come in your life. Imagine the experiences you are yet to have — the possibilities yet to unfold. Hang on. Don't sell yourself short.
- » As stressful as this is in the moment, remember you have equal and opposite positive emotions vying for your attention, enjoyable possibilities that will excite you and bring joy to your heart with the people you love, and the people who love you.

Reduce Your Risk

I promise that if you are willing to speak up, ask for help, and focus on your own well-being, things will get better.

Remember: While it may seem as if these suicidal thoughts and feelings are everlasting, they are *never* a permanent condition. You *will* feel better again. In the meantime, here are some ways to cope and hopefully dispel your suicidal thoughts and feelings:

» Engage in face-to-face interaction with someone every day. I know you feel like isolating yourself and being completely alone, but this is not healthy. Connect and get involved. Ask friends or family to spend time with you. If you need to call the crisis helpline to talk about your feelings, that is OK too.

» Have a safety plan. Have a plan of action that you can follow during a suicidal crisis. This plan should contain the phone numbers for your doctor, your therapist, the suicide helpline, friends, or family; anyone who can help in an emergency. Print it out; keep a copy on your phone. I use a great app called Evernote for note-taking and other important information.

» Have a written schedule. Routine and structure are very important. Stick to the schedule, no matter what. Make sure you add self-care, even if it's for only a few minutes. Say no when you have to because maintaining a stable schedule is more important.

» Sun and light are your friends — go outdoors to enjoy nature and direct sunlight for thirty minutes a day. Take in fresh air and the beautiful landscape that surrounds you. Embrace this experience and find gratitude in these little things that so many of us take for granted.

» Exercise, eat right, and get your rest. This will help ease your anxiety and emotions. I recommend at least thirty minutes of exercise, but if that seems too big a mountain, start small. Can you do ten minutes of exercise, three times a day? Can you go for a twenty-minute walk? Yes, you can do it! As for eating right, choose a well-balanced and healthy diet (avoid too much sugar). And ensure that you get at least seven to eight hours of uninterrupted sleep each night.

» Make time for things that bring you happiness. I know it might seem like nothing could possibly bring you any happiness, but you must force yourself to find something that brings you a little joy.

» Remember your self-care. You need to acknowledge that you are what is most important, especially at these moments. Perhaps you have fallen away from taking care of yourself. This is a great time to establish new habits for self-care and rewrite your goals.

» Avoid anything that can make you feel worse. This includes songs that remind you of sad situations or times, looking at photographs that bring up sad memories, listening to depressing music, or anything that triggers sad feelings or thoughts.

» Adhere to a plan. Follow a treatment plan, go to follow-up appointments, take medications as instructed and prescribed by a licensed medical professional.

» Avoid alcohol and illegal drugs. (Self-medicating is a no-no.)

» Connect with your family. Involve your family in all treatment. Invite them to counseling/therapy sessions.

» Keep a gratitude journal: Focus on the good things in life (talk therapy methods may also help you achieve this).

» Be proactive. Remove guns, knives, and dangerous drugs in the household.

» Develop a tool kit. Seek out things that you enjoy, such as engaging with friends and family you enjoy being with. Surround yourself with fond memories, happy pictures, and things that inspire you.

» Attend self-help/support groups. Surround yourself with like-minded people. Sharing the anguish and anxieties that drive you toward suicidal ideation can be a relief and bring you comfort. You will see how others got through it. If you can support other people, you may feel better about yourself and those around you.

Take Immediate Action

Step #1: Promise Not to Act on Emotion

A time-out is in order. You're overwhelmed right now. Give yourself some distance between your thoughts and the desire to act on them. Make this promise to yourself: "I will wait twenty-four hours and won't do anything during that time." Then you can add more time to your goal and make it thirty-six, seventy-two, or ninety-six hours. Keep that promise.

Thoughts are one thing and actions are another. Suicidal thoughts do not have to end with suicide. Life is a journey, not a race. There is no timetable or deadline to feeling better. Just wait. Be patient. Give it some time and put some distance between what you are thinking and what you might want to act on.

Step #2: Avoid Recreational Drugs and Alcohol

Do not self-medicate. This is a red flag, and I urge you to take this seriously. You don't do drugs — drugs do you. Your desperate thoughts can become heightened if you take drugs or drink alcohol. Drugs and alcohol are never a good idea, especially when you feel hopeless or are thinking about suicide. This is reckless behavior. Take a time-out and avoid being reckless.

Step #3: The Safety Net of Home

Home is where you are probably most safe, but there are things at home that you can use to harm yourself. Pills, knives, razors, guns – these all need to be removed from your home. Go somewhere where you can feel safe. You don't want to be alone during this time.

It's best to be with someone you love and care about and who loves and cares about you. Even if you don't talk, just being together is enough. If you are on prescription medications, entrust somebody who can administer them to you responsibly and according to your prescriptions.

Thinking about suicide is not necessarily wrong or alarming, but if you are considering harming yourself or harming others, *that* is a huge red flag, and an indication your thoughts are unhealthy and need to be addressed with a mental health professional. If this is the case, don't over-react; you should talk to a trusted adult immediately and let them bring you to a mental health professional. Having someone with you will make you feel comfortable and safe. You are not in trouble. You should not feel like you are crazy. There are many possible causes: chemical imbalance, neurotransmitters and neurons not connecting, wrong medication, stress, thoughts of being a burden or alone, and so much more. If these thoughts are really strong and you are in need of immediate help, call 911 or have somebody take you to the emergency room ASAP. It is imperative for you *not* to be alone.

Step #4: Do Not Keep Suicidal Thoughts and Feelings to Yourself
It's best to share your heart with others. The first step in coping with suicidal thoughts and feelings is to share them with someone you trust. For me, it was my grandmother, and now it's my counselor. For you, it might be a parent, a coach, a teacher, your friends, your friends' parents, a guidance counselor, or a youth pastor. You have people who care about you and would do anything to help you, but they can't help if they don't know. Say something. Take the first step. You need to be willing to open up and share.

During this time, you can't let fear, shame, or embarrassment get in the way of opening up and talking to somebody.

Step #5: Don't Ever Lose Hope

It will be OK. I promise.

I lost all hope, but I had my grandmother, Mickey; she was there for me. I'm glad I wasn't afraid to open up and talk to her. You will survive these feelings. Have hope. Believe. Be willing to speak up and reach out. I know that it worked for me and hundreds of people I've met. I know it will work for you. These feelings will subside. Tomorrow will be a new day.

Give yourself the time you need and don't fight this battle alone.

Get out your journal, diary, a piece of paper, or a notecard. Go on. I'll wait.

Do you have a pencil or pen? You need that, too.

OK, are you ready?

Write down the answers to these questions:

1. Who are your trusted adults?
2. What is your self-care plan?

Teachers are so important. It's about

RELATIONSHIPS.

CHAPTER 11

PREVENTING SUICIDE

"Each one of us can make a difference.
Together we make change."

- BARBARA MIKULSKI

I began working with communities before I got my full education and became certified in suicide prevention and crisis intervention. I don't think one can have enough education, especially in the areas of mental health. Just like in the Marine Corps, on-the-job training proves more valuable. I am proud of my education, but nothing could have furnished me with the tools I need for my work as much as my time in the trenches — helping thousands of teens and being of service to school communities across the nation and around the world.

My career is my passion, but it can be gut-wrenchingly sad and difficult at times. It's especially demanding when I am called on to meet with parents after the loss of their child to suicide. It's grueling to assist communities during a suicide contagion, a loss due to a car wreck, or some other kind of crisis in their community. However, I'm good at this. I appreciate the opportunity to help others deal with their pain. I love being real with young people; I love sharing my own experiences as well as listening to their hearts. Sometimes, just listening to them makes them feel so much better. Maybe that is what they need. They need me just to listen and validate their feelings. I'm really OK with that. Whatever I can do for them; I'm happy to be their support and encouragement.

Over the years, I have expanded my knowledge base regarding the psychology of suicide. However, I regard my hands-on experience — coupled with my years in therapy — as my greatest education. I wouldn't trade my personal involvement for anything. No other educational resources have prepared me as well for this work. I am very grateful to God for blessing me with the ability and passion to provide this service for others.

The first formal training I received was from a Seattle-based psychologist, Dr. Paul Quinnett, a leading gatekeeper in the field of suicide prevention. His Question, Persuade, and Refer (QPR) program is a leading training resource in the field. A gatekeeper, according to the Surgeon General's Strategy for Suicide Prevention, is someone in a position to recognize a crisis as well as the warning signs that someone may be contemplating suicide.

I love the simplicity of Quinnett's QPR program, but I wasn't sure how it related to my work with teens. Teens are a whole different breed. In this chapter, I am going to share what QPR has taught me, but I am adding some additional details based on my understanding of teens.

There are important things to know in order to prevent a suicide. If you are not clear regarding the facts about suicide, you may hesitate to act and help save a life. Separating what you might have heard from the truth is essential. By doing so, you will be able to recognize those in crisis and be confident that the individual suffering gets the help they need.

Making Sense of Myths and Facts

If someone shares suicidal thoughts with you, they are pleading for help. Try to get them to talk about their feelings. Don't judge them, just listen. And please, seek help immediately.

If they make you promise not to tell anyone, remember that their life is worth more than that promise, so if things get out of control, share with someone else. You need to be there for your loved one and that means doing what is best for them — including getting others involved if needed. Encourage them to create a plan and open up about their thoughts and feelings. Again, seek professional help immediately, call 911, tell a trusted adult, parents, etc. Do not take matters into your own hands. Do not think you can be the one to save their life. Do not consider the situation just a normal "attention getting, drama filled" episode from a teenager. I can't say it enough, take all signs seriously and seek help immediately.

Your intervening is the first step in persuading an individual to get the help they need. You could start the conversation that saves a life. It doesn't matter what is a myth and what is a fact — provide help, right away.

How you ask the question isn't as important as the fact that you *ask* the question:

Are you suicidal?

What?

Discussing suicide is an opportunity for communication. Just because you ask if someone is suicidal doesn't mean you are encouraging suicide. It's one of the first steps toward inspiring a suicidal person to live. Talking about feelings can diminish the crisis and lower anxiety and fears. Don't be afraid to ask; don't be afraid to start the conversation. Talking about suicide might be a plea for help.

However, those at greater risk will exhibit signs beyond suicidal talk. Remember, many suicide attempts are the result of a situation gone wrong and the individual thinking it's the end of the world. To that end, one of the best things you can do is assist the young person by developing a safety plan. Helpful safety plans include spending time with family and friends, checking in with trusted adults, and creating a plan of action for the future. Simply discussing who and what is on a safety plan contributes to positive feelings, hopefully clearing the black cloud a bit more.

When?

Nobody is suicidal at *all* times. The risk of suicide for any person varies across time as circumstances change. Regular risk assessments are important for individuals who are in jeopardy. And while it's a common belief that suicides occur predominantly during the winter months when the weather is poor, most suicides happen during the spring and early summer months.

Who?

Suicide often runs in the family. While suicide may be over represented in one household, it isn't necessarily inherited. Families share the same emotional environment, and the completed suicide of one family member may well raise the awareness of suicide as an option for other family members.

Of course, those who have attempted suicide once are regarded as high risk to attempt again. It is very likely that the level of danger will increase with each subsequent suicide attempt. It is in the three months following an attempted suicide when a person is most at-risk for completing a suicide. While there might be a sudden improvement in a person's mental state following an attempt, this could also mean the person has made a decision to die by suicide and feels better because of the decision. This is a very fragile time period and weekly mental health counseling should be implemented and taken seriously.

Everyone has the potential for suicide. Evidence shows that those with predisposing conditions (depression, substance abuse, emotional pain, etc.) are *more likely* to attempt or complete a suicide, but suicide excludes no one.

The friends and family of those who die by suicide often say their loved one exhibited no visible signs. It is possible that the signs just weren't recognized. Attempted or completed suicides usually provide warnings and red flags up to two weeks prior to the forever decision.

Why?

Suicidal young people are *not* insane or mentally ill. Suicidal adolescents tend to appear unhappy; they may be classified as having a mood disorder such as depression, but most are not legally insane. Of course, there are some exceptions to that statement; there is a small number of individuals whose mental state meets psychiatric criteria for mental illness and who need psychiatric help. Regarding depression, it's undeniably a contributing factor in many suicides, but not all. Not all suicidal people are depressed.

We all suffer rejection at some point in our lives, though. A suicide can be precipitated by the loss of a relationship — romantic, familial, or even business related. Suicide seduces people from all races, religions, walks of life, and socioeconomic status.

How?

I know it's hard, but truly — no promises should be kept if you are concerned about a person being suicidal. Even if someone makes you swear not to tell, you have to consider that person's life more important than a confidence. No letters or notes should remain unopened or unread. If there is a potential for self-harm, then confidentiality cannot be maintained, nor should it be. A person not thinking clearly needs a trusted friend or adult to think *for* them and make the right decisions. This is the responsibility of a friend or trusted adult.

Evidence shows that some suicidal people share their thoughts and plans with at least one friend or family member. Adolescents are more likely to 'ask' for help through non-verbal gestures than to express their situation verbally. This is why it is important to know the signs and to be aware of red flags.

Effective intervention for suicide comes from all people who interact with a suicidal person by way of emotional support and encouragement. Don't think the only effective intervention comes from medical professionals or psychotherapists with extensive experience in the area of suicidal behavior.

When someone intervenes with a suicidal young person, it is common that the individual is defensive, and resists help at first. However, these behaviors are often a barrier imposed to test how much people care and how prepared they are to help. For most adolescents considering suicide, it is a relief to have someone genuinely care about them. It is a relief to share the emotional burden with another person. When questioned some time later, the vast majority express gratitude for the intervention.

How Much?

All suicide attempts must be treated seriously as the person has or had the intent to die. Do not dismiss a suicide attempt as simply someone seeking attention. It *is* likely the person has tried to gain attention and, therefore, this attention is needed. The attention that they get may well save their lives.

Suicidal people can be talked out of taking immediate action; they can certainly help themselves. A suicidal person has a distorted perception of reality; they cannot seem to fathom potential solutions to their problems. With the proper support and constructive assistance from caring and informed people, a young person can gain full self-direction and self-management in their lives.

Suicides *can* be prevented; the perceived crisis will not last forever. People *can* help. Let's save lives and get the help the individual needs.

Signs Someone Might be Suicidal

Here are some signs that are easy to miss; they are red flags and need to be taken seriously. In most cases of completed or attempted suicides, signs are present, but unrecognizable. If a person in crisis isn't talking about their thoughts or feelings than nobody knows they're hurting. If nobody knows they're hurting then nobody is looking for signs or clues that something is wrong.

If we know the signs or know what to look for, there can be different endings to many stories. We need to educate ourselves and our schools on the red flags and what to look for in our young people. This is our responsibility in today's world where teen suicide is an epidemic.

Here are the most common signs that someone might be suicidal. Recognizing these clues could help you save a life:

 Suicidal Talk
This talk of suicide might just suggest that a person is planning or considering a forever decision. Any talk of suicide should be taken seriously. This could be a cry for help and should be addressed immediately. Your job here is to ask further questions and know what to do next.

Unease about the Future
Who really knows what their future holds and what they want to do with their lives? So much has changed over the past ten to fifteen years with technological advancements coupled with teens scientifically maturing later. If you hear comments about being

perfect, unease about who they are, or uncertainty about what the future has in store — you should recognize this as a potential sign. You have to ask more questions and address this as a serious red flag.

3 Parting with Prized Possessions

If a friend or someone you know is giving away stuff or possessions, this is a red flag. Address it and don't be afraid to ask *why*. When someone is suicidal, they often start to think about getting rid of their stuff because they know they will not need it when they're dead. Some see it as closure and think it will make their grieving friends or family have comfort in their death.

4 Obtaining a Weapon

This isn't always alarming (especially if you live in a rural area where hunting is permitted), but if you recognize other signs along with the red flag of obtaining a weapon, this could be a sign someone is suicidal. Also, if your friend isn't a person who has shown interest in weapons and all of a sudden has a curiosity, it's worth investigating.

5 Changes in Sleep Patters

A person who is suicidal has inconsistent sleep patterns. This is because the individual is restless and stressed. If you notice this behavior, please approach them in a calm, nonjudgmental manner and try to get them to open up to you.

Drug or Alcohol Abuse

Self-medicating or abusing drugs or alcohol can be a sign a person is depressed or thinking of suicide. Sometimes this drug use or heavy drinking is their way to escape reality. Most people who take their lives have drugs or alcohol in their system at the time of their death. This is a common red flag.

Low Motivation and Lack of Social Interaction

When a person is suicidal, they might no longer take an interest in their social life. They isolate themselves, cutting off friends and family, thinking they are not good enough. They don't think they need a social life. They don't think they are worthy of being around other people.

Self-Harm

This is the biggest warning sign that someone is suicidal. Many people "test the waters" — harming themselves to see if they are actually capable of going through with suicide. Former self-harmers also say that physical pain serves as an extreme way to get their mind off emotional pain.

Risky Behavior

Suicidal people tend to take more risks, like picking fights or driving recklessly.

Past Suicide Attempts

This is called "suicidal tendencies." Depression isn't something that is easily cured. Even if someone seems to be on the road to mental well-being, a missed dose of a prescribed medication or an ineffective medication might cause a person to attempt suicide again. Try to look for other warning signs that would indicate that they may once again be suicidal.

Body Language
Slumped shoulders, staring at the ground, and an unwillingness to make eye contact could be an indication that a person is depressed. This is a very typical sign. Combined with other red flags, this could indicate that someone is suffering from depression or suicidal thoughts. If a person suddenly adopts this body language, it could be a sign that they are suicidal.

Happiness and Calmness
This one is hard to detect. Many people think that when you hit your lowest point of depression, you will actually follow through with suicide. But that is not always true. When you are depressed and you have hit that low point, you may spend most of the day in bed, unwilling to do anything. Suicide takes energy and planning. When someone attempts suicide, it can happen when they are just above that low point and have the energy to create and execute a plan.

Just before some people attempt suicide, they appear happy and calm. I suspect it's because they have their mind made up and their plan finalized. To them, the completion of suicide will end their pain and suffering. Teens don't realize that although their pain is gone, it is only the beginning for their friends, family, and loved one.

Take all Signs Seriously

The more dangerous and definite the plan, the greater the suicide risk. Be calm, reassuring, and supportive. Be patient, and don't blame. Don't make promises. Don't hold a secret that might result in death.

Talk through some steps that will prevent imminent physical harm. Help work out a plan with them to ensure their ongoing safety. If they refuse your help, then seek additional help immediately. Call 911 or go to the nearest emergency room. You can also call any of the resources in the back of this book.

When the person is safe, find someone to talk to for your own well-being. Don't underestimate the importance of what you did and the impact the conversation had on you. You also need support. Take care of yourself.

CHAPTER 12

SUICIDE AND GOD

> *"The essence of all religions is one.*
> *Only their approaches are different."*
>
> - MAHATMA GANDHI

Before I go any further, I'd like to clarify one thing: I personally believe in one God and I am a Christian, but I respect all religions. It doesn't matter to me if you are Jewish, Catholic, Protestant, Buddhist, Islamic, Hindu, or Agnostic; I love you all the same.

OK, moving on…

When I am in a community presenting to the parents, I often hear how we need to bring God back into American schools. While I don't disagree, we cannot rely on God to solve all our problems Himself.

If you had cancer, would you pray to God without going to see a doctor? Would you skip chemotherapy or radiation sessions and simply rely on God for healing? Didn't God give us doctors for a reason? If you are a person of faith, I'm pretty sure you would pray for a positive outcome, but I am also sure that you would seek appropriate medical attention.

It's the same with teen mental health: if you are suffering, please see a professional *and* pray.

That being said, I would like to dive deeper into the relationship between suicide and God, specifically the theory that suicide is an unforgiveable sin that results in an eternity of damnation.

Suicide – Heaven or Hell?

When a community brings me in after a loss, my schedule often includes meeting with the local youth pastors, senior pastors, and church members. Many religious leaders are very vocal in their beliefs, and I am OK with that, but I am also cautious about imposing personal philosophies on teens at such a young age. I'd like our students to learn about a variety of world religions before they deem themselves a believer of one faith over another. I want our youth to develop their own values, morals, and beliefs — by way of trusted influences, positive support and encouragement, and meaningful conversations.

One particular night, I attended a "Stump the Pastor" session where folks asked questions to test the mettle of the minister in attendance.

The inevitable question surfaced, "Is suicide a sin?"

The pastor responded with a resounding YES! He also went on to say that he thought it would be hard for someone who died by suicide to make it into Heaven, and that anybody professing to be a Christian wouldn't do harm to themselves. To a true Christian, he said, the prospect of suicide is unthinkable and simply not something a Christian would do.

I was taken aback by this, and quite frankly a little perturbed, especially because we were talking to teens and parents about mental health. I need to say this: Let's not stress too much over the theology of the question. Following a death, there is a family hurting that needs your love, compassion, and unconditional support.

What does the phrase "true Christian" really mean? Doesn't God work with each of us where we are? We are all at different points in our journey. We have different weaknesses, problems, and perspectives. It is your faith or belief that makes you a Christian. It's not up to us to sit in judgment of the faith of another or to proclaim one person a true Christian to the exclusion of another. Only God can judge their faith and their faith is all that really matters as they stand before God and Jesus.

I believe that God decides where we go and when we die; the judgment is His alone. God makes that call based on the choices we make and the condition of our hearts while we walk the earth. I suspect that we will be surprised to see certain people in Heaven. I also suspect that we will be equally surprised when others are absent. In my opinion, this pastor was not responsible in regards to his influence. Our young people are so impressionable. Perhaps it would have been better for him simply to encourage his audience to form a better relationship with God. This community was hurting, and he could have been more understanding, compassionate, and gentle with the teens he was attempting to bring closer to God.

Isn't a sin a sin? Does one act of sin make any other act of sin worse?

In the Bible, Paul states, "I die daily." This means he sins daily, buy he knows where forgiveness lies.

Paul also affirms in Acts 16:31 that in order to get to Heaven, all you have to do is "believe in the Lord Jesus, and you will be saved — you and your household."

The only thing that keeps us from Heaven is disbelief, nothing else. Mental illness is a complex issue, and God understands this. None of us has the right to determine God's will.

God does not want any of His children to be in pain. Suicide is a forever decision based on depression or other psychiatric conditions. It can also be due to a lack of love, debilitating stress, not wanting to be a burden, or the feeling of being alone. God loves everyone, especially loves those who suffer. Wouldn't it stand to reason that we should then be supportive of those who need help and applaud them for stepping up and asking for that help?

I don't like "Stump the Pastor" night; the term implies that the minister has all the answers and that his answers are all correct. This particular pastor needed to be less of a clergyman and more of a trusted adult for these young, impressionable teens that had recently suffered an unimaginable loss.

We can manipulate scripture to argue just about anything we like, but to do so is wrong. God grieves the loss of any person the same as he grieves the death of His Son.

Teenagers should know that those who harm themselves or die by suicide are crying out for help and searching for answers to the pain they feel.

I pray that our youth, especially those suffering, will find the trusted adults they need in their lives to help guide them toward what is best.

Let's all do what is right when guiding our teens.

13 REASONS WHY: WHAT YOU NEED TO KNOW AND MY TWO CENTS

I'd like to share with you my thoughts on the popular Netflix series, *13 Reasons Why*.

About the Show

This show captured the attention of youth all over the world and generated many discussions among teens, families, and schools regarding issues like suicide prevention, mental health, bullying, and more. However, mental health professionals, advocacy groups, and suicide prevention experts worry about whether the series presents risks to viewers because of how the show addresses some of the important and complicated issues youth face today.

The response to season one was alarming, and this caused the producers and the executives at Netflix to make some changes — specifically, they added a statement at the beginning of season two. Cast members warn viewers about the heavy content as well as provide a de facto invitation to open up dialogue.

> *"By shedding a light on these difficult topics, we hope our show can help viewers start a conversation."*
>
> *- 13 REASONS WHY*

But is this enough to encourage struggling viewers to reach out and ask for help, especially after binge-watching the show? In my professional and personal opinion, I don't think so. The directors don't care enough about the viewers. If they did, they would have added the necessary helplines or instructed viewers *how* to ask for help in the closing or opening sections.

The second season provides more warnings, but it is not enough. I'd like to see the show really spend time helping people who are hurting and who are triggered by the show's content. Is it their responsibility? No, it isn't one hundred percent their responsibility. Parents need to be aware of the dangers of this show. Parents should watch *13 Reasons Why* with their kids so they can discuss the topics and help their children process it appropriately. Considering the popularity of the show, however, I am disappointed that the network didn't take a more prominent stance on providing life-saving resources for their audience.

Season two has been released, and many teens are going back to watch season one again. I want to strongly encourage parents, educators, coaches, and all trusted adults to understand the severity of the topics covered in this show and the emotional stress it could take on our teens.

In season two, Hannah Baker goes down a path that significantly impacts her mentally and emotionally, culminating in her suicide. Clay Jensen, her friend, is left to deal with the pieces and attempt to learn about the painful events that led to Hannah's decision. This is all very real and raw; the directors did a great job telling the story. What they neglected to do is assist the viewer who could easily be triggered.

The show takes an honest, graphic look at the issues our youth face today, so please know that the visuals could upset your child. It can certainly be valuable to watch it, even if you yourself struggle with mental illness, but parents should take an active role. Engage in discussions about the show, differentiating between fiction and reality, and watch your child carefully to see what impact the topics have on them. If you are concerned at any point, address it immediately. An organization called SAVE (Suicide Awareness Voices of Education) gathered resources from over seventy-five experts in various fields to create the *13 Reasons Why Toolkit*, which you can find on this website: 13reasonswhytoolkit.org.

The show highlights many issues prevalent in today's world: sexual assault, suicide, gun violence, bullying, substance abuse, and more. It's important for people to talk about how the show makes them feel. It's important to encourage ongoing conversations among families and in schools.

While I am concerned about the potential harm resulting from watching *13 Reasons Why*, I am heartened by the fact that the show is forcing us to talk — and this conversation is long overdue.

Sexual Assault – A Concerning Topic

Just turn on the television. We see stories daily exposing people in our government, celebrities, and others as alleged sexual predators. It's good that we are making headway; it's good that we have the Me Too movement. No means no. No person should ever be subjected to sexual assault or rape. Unfortunately, it happens every day in the work place, on college campuses, and even in our schools.

Sexual assault or unwanted sexual contact is wrong, and *13 Reasons Why* has several episodes covering this very theme.

This is another great example of when you can have a meaningful discussion with your teen about right and wrong. These scenes and conversations can help teens come forward and share experiences they may have hidden before.

13 Reasons Why provides content where we are given the opportunity to discuss difficult issues with our teens such as consent, ongoing harassment, and peer pressure. Instead of bashing the show, let's look at the positives. We need to stop living under a rock, thinking these issues don't happen in our communities. They do. I can assure you they do. This show offers an opportunity for real-life dialogue and meaningful, open relationships between trusted adults and children.

FINAL THOUGHTS

I have worked with teens for more than twenty-five years all over the world. As you know, mental health is near and dear to my heart and I proudly live with mental illness every day. My faith is very important to me, and I strive to be the man God intends for me to be. I take great comfort in my relationship with my higher power.

My hope is that we remove the dogmatic scare tactics and condemnation when we talk to our youth about suicide — that they will go to hell if they die by suicide. Frightening our children with threats of hell to try to make them think twice about suicide and self-harm is irresponsible and foolish. I am deeply concerned about this.

As a professional suicide prevention trainer and teen and family communicator, I am all for saving lives, but there is a better way to address this issue. Scare tactics only lead to pain and confusion. Openness, communication without judgment, support, and unconditional love are the catalysts for our teens to get the help they so desperately need.

Let's remove the stigma once and for all. Let's get comfortable with being uncomfortable as we talk openly about suicide. Let's usher in a new era of openness on the subject of mental illness and do our part to educate others. We can reverse what threatens to become the greatest public health crisis of our time.

QUIZ - DO YOU HAVE SIGNS OF DEPRESSION?

Take a moment. Be honest with yourself. Read these questions carefully. Analyze yourself. Your life. Your feelings. If you relate to any of the situations below, this could be a red flag and the first indication that you should talk to a mental health professional. Do not be afraid to speak up and reach out. You are surrounded by people who love you and want to help you. Let them.

1. Do you live with a family member who suffers from depression?

Whether it is environmental or genetic, studies have shown that living with a mother, father, or other blood relative who has depression increases your risk of developing depression.

2. Does life feel pointless?

Perhaps you might feel hopeless on occasion as you forge ahead in life or in school. Does this feeling of hopelessness persist day after day and affect your behavior? This could be a sign of depression.

3. Do you have trouble concentrating?

If you struggle with concentration when you're reading or watching something you enjoy, you could be depressed.

4. Have you withdrawn from your friends and family?

I get that you're cool and parents are not. I get that your time is valuable and your friends cause drama. I'm the same way. I also like to be alone and chill. However, time with your friends and family is very important. Social bonding or social interaction is good for you and your overall well-being. You learn coping skills, problem-solving skills, raise your self-esteem, and you're less likely to make bad choices. If you turn down opportunities to be with friends and family to be alone and isolating yourself, you might be depressed.

5. Have you noticed something different about your weight lately?

Maybe you've put on a few pounds or you've lost weight without intentionally trying to. There might be more to this than you think. Weight loss or weight gain could be a symptom of depression. Perhaps you have no appetite or find yourself seeking comfort food. Your brain may be experiencing a change in chemistry as a result of being depressed.

6. Do you have trouble sleeping or are you sleeping too much?

I know you're exhausted from everything. Adulting sucks. Homework takes up too much time. School starts too early. Social media takes up a lot of time too, but we won't talk about that being a hindrance in your life, right? Teens and adults should get at least eight hours of uninterrupted sleep a night. Sleep is very important. I also know you probably don't get enough sleep. If you go through periods of sleeplessness or periods of sleeping too much, depression could be the cause.

7. Do you have physical pain that won't go away?

Depression isn't just pain from emotions. Depression can also manifest itself in the form of physical pain that persists, even though your doctor has not found a reason for it. This could be a sign of depression resulting from a chemical imbalance in your brain that makes you perceive the pain differently.

8. Have your grades taken a nosedive? Have you stopped participating in extracurricular activities you once enjoyed?

Depression's best friends are apathy and lack of energy. This dangerous duo can do serious damage to your performance in school and negatively impact other daily activities. This is depression, my friend. But, with professional help and understanding, you can live a healthy life. If your passion for activities you once enjoyed has faded away, depression could be the reason why.

9. Are you having suicidal thoughts?

If you are thinking about harming yourself or others, this is a red flag. If you have thoughts of suicide, this is a red flag. Immediately ask a trusted adult for help. Immediately seek help from a mental health professional. If you know of a friend who is having suicidal thoughts, please speak up and say something. It's the right thing to do. Your friend is not thinking clearly, and you need to step in and help.

You might think it's shameful or wrong to have suicidal thoughts. We are only human and thoughts like this might cross our minds from time to time. If these thoughts persist, it could be a signal that it's time for you to seek the help you need. Listen: You are not alone. Help is just an ask away.

When you make the decision to ask for help and show up for an initial medical assessment, you can expect proper medical care and treatment from a mental health professional. You will likely start to feel better, and thoughts of suicide will dissipate. When you're suffering from depression, it seems as if nothing will make you feel better — but I can assure you that you will. Little by little, day by day. Sometimes, it's minute-by-minute and one breath to another. Do the work and you'll be very thankful you didn't make a forever decision. I am, and I am thankful I continue to do the work daily.

This is the time for you to be courageous and trust the process.

My favorite words during difficult times are, "It *will* be OK. I can get through this." It *will* be OK and you will get through this. I know you can. Have patience in the process. Don't make any decisions based on emotion. There are plenty of resources to help you get back to your old self. Talk to your doctor. Ask questions and remember that it is okay to take a TIME-OUT and make some changes for a day or two.

If you answered "Yes!" to any of the questions above, **you need to talk to somebody.** Don't try to get better without help and support or think that life isn't worth living. Please start the conversation. Open your heart. There is nothing to be ashamed of. I know you'll be proud you did.

APPENDIX

Resources: Speak Up ; Reach Out!

Find support and services for yourself or others through these resources and advocacy organizations:

||||||||||||||||||||||||||||||||||||||||||||||||||||||||||||||||||||

Suicide Prevention: 800-273-TALK (8255)
American Foundation for Suicide Prevention — Talking Saves Lives!

Your call will automatically be routed to a trained crisis worker who will listen. This person care and will direct you to mental health services in your area. The service is free and confidential and open 24/7. Keep this number in your smartphone under ICE (In Case of Emergency).

Teen Line: 310-855-HOPE or 800-TLC-TEEN
Sometimes teens want to just talk with other teens. This is a great place to start. It's all about teens helping teens. Teen Line is a national hotline designed to help teenagers acknowledge and deal with their issues before they become overwhelmingly difficult to address.

Call this number before you're overwhelmed and a situation becomes a crisis. This is a safe number to call and I highly recommend it.

This hotline is open from 6 p.m. to 10 p.m. PST every night. After hours, your call will be directed to Didi Hirsh's Suicide Prevention Center.

The Trevor Project: Trevor Life Line (crisis line for LGBTQ youth) 866-488-7386 | TrevorText 202-304-1200
The Trevor Life Line is a 24/7 confidential hotline for anyone ex-periencing a crisis or suicidal thoughts. It was specifically de-veloped to help LGBTQ youth.

Text line is available Monday to Friday between 3pm–10pm EST/noon–7 pm PST. Standard text messaging rates apply.

Depression: National Institute of Mental Health:
www.NIMH.NIH.gov
Transforming the understanding and treatment of mental illnesses.

Anxiety: Anxiety and Depression Association of America:
www.adaa.org
Anxiety and Depression Association of America

National Eating Disorders Association: 800-931-2237
www.NationalEatingDisorders.org
This national helpline offers support for youth struggling with any type of eating disorder.

StopBullying.gov
www.StopBullying.gov
Bullying is a problem with any age group; parents and schools can help. Learn how to stop bullying by visiting the stop bullying website for great resources.

Substance Abuse Hotline: 800-662-4357
www.SAMHSA.gov
This confidential 24/7 hotline offers information and treatment options for individuals facing mental and/or substance abuse disorders.

National STD and AIDS Hotline: 800-227-8922
www.ASHASTD.ord
This hotline offers information and resources for anyone facing (or concerned about) AIDS or any other sexually transmitted disease.

National Child Abuse Hotline:
800-4-A-CHILD (800-422-4453)
This 24/7 hotline offers crisis intervention and support in over 170 languages for victims of child abuse, or those who suspect the abuse of others.

The American Foundation for Suicide Prevention: 800-273-8255
If you or anyone you know is having suicidal thoughts, this is a great place to call. This foundation provides great information, resources, and crisis intervention.

National Alliance of Mental Illness (NAMI) Helpline: 800-950-NAMI (6264)
This hotline provides support, information, and referrals to anyone suffering from mental illness.

Crisis Text Line: 741741
When you just want to text, help is only a text away.

PTSD Hotline: 800-273-8255
Whether you know you suffer from PTSD or suspect you may suffer from a traumatic injury, this number is a safe space for you to reach out and talk.

RAINN - Rape, Abuse & Incest National Network - National Sexual Assault Hotline: 800-656-HOPE (4673)
www.rainn.org
FREE. Confidential. 24/7

If someone touches you in a way that's not okay or shows you something that makes you feel like you are not safe, you don't have to keep it a secret. It's not right, and it's not your fault.

Find local support. RAINN partners with more than a thousand local sexual assault service providers across the country that can provide support in your community.

Substance Abuse Prevention and Education: DARE
www.DARE.org

National Institute on Drug Abuse for Teens:
www.teens.drugabuse.gov

Alcohol Abuse: National Institute on Alcohol Abuse and Alcoholism:
www.niaaa.nih.gov

TheGriefGirl.com
www.thegriefgirl.com
Resources, podcasts, and materials on depression, mental illness, grief and suicide from a certified grief counselor and health educator.

BEFORE YOU GO

It is possible. If you speak up ; if you reach out – you can find happiness. The following letter is from a young lady who contemplated suicide, but found the help she needed. If she can do it, so can you.

You are loved.

> *Suicide is a permanent answer to a temporary problem."*
> *Simple words, but the reason I am where I am today.*

The first time I heard Jeff speak, I was fifteen — the poster child for a happy, healthy, loved teen; except for recently losing my dad after a battle with cancer. There was an outpouring of love from friends and family. I accepted their sentiments, but never truly let myself grieve. Exteriorly, I kept up the image of healing, while internally I spiraled downward into a deep depression; I knew I was in trouble. On that day, Jeff captured the heart of my school, but it was one phrase about suicide that stuck with me — 'suicide is a permanent answer to a temporary problem.' I thought, "but my problem IS permanent — the loss of my father." I typed an email to Jeff, explaining how my situation did not fit; an attempt to justify that suicide might be an OK option. I never intended to send it, but it felt good writing out my 'secret' thoughts. Thankfully, I did send that email and Jeff immediately set motion to getting me help.

Through later conversations with Jeff, my family, and friends, I realized that my problem was not the loss of my father, but the engulfing depression. It was the mild anxiety I had always experienced but was amplified with this loss. It was mental illness that I needed to face and address. I discovered I actually had SO much to live for and I vowed to live each day with passion and appreciation. I won't say that it's been smooth sailing since. Later, I faced depression and an eating disorder, but was able to work through these by keeping Jeff's lessons in mind.

Jeff is an amazing human who has the unique ability to reach into the hearts of the young and old. He emboldens those too scared to admit they need help and guides those who seek to help others. In a world plagued by increasing violence — both self-directed and outward, Jeff's message of acceptance, perseverance, and passion/belief in humanity is needed more than ever.

Today, I am a healthy woman and a successful veterinarian, getting ready to marry the woman of my dreams; living a life of adventure surrounded by friends and family whom I love. I live each day with the goal of brightening the day of those around me — you never know when one smile, open door, or friendly stranger can remind someone that they are worthwhile, that whatever problem they are facing is temporary and it gets better.

– ERIN DUSH, D.V.M

Made in the USA
San Bernardino, CA
03 December 2019

60791449R00122